garden mosaics

garden mosaics

19 beautiful mosaic projects for your garden

Emma Biggs and **Tessa Hunkin**

St. Martin's Griffin
New York

Library of Congress Cataloging-in-Publication Data Available Upon
Request

ISBN-13: 978-0-312-56204-5
ISBN-10: 0-312-56204-7

First U.S. Edition: May 2009

Senior Editor: Corinne Masciocchi
Designer: Peter Crump
Photographer: Shona Wood
Production: Marion Storz
Editorial Direction: Rosemary Wilkinson

2 4 6 8 10 9 7 5 3 1

Reproduction by Colourscan Overseas Co Pte Ltd, Singapore
Printed and bound by Craft Print International Ltd, Singapore

contents

introduction

introduction

Mosaic is a fascinating and distinctive form of art and decoration. It has a long and glorious history that is still visible in the great mosaics of the Classical and Byzantine worlds, and their remarkable preservation is evidence of the durability and permanence of mosaic art. These same qualities make it an ideal technique for use in outdoor situations where other art forms, such as painting or ceramics, would quickly fade and crumble. This book aims to provide all the information necessary to make outdoor mosaics that will survive the challenges of the weather and add interest and delight to the garden. Mosaics can be used to decorate areas of paving and paths, or to add color to walls throughout the year, complementing the surrounding plants in summer and providing a visual focus during the dull, bare days of winter. Mosaic can also be used to great effect on three-dimensional objects, such as seats, pots and sculptures.

The book is arranged around a series of step-by-step projects that offer a wide variety of applications and techniques. There are simple projects suitable for complete beginners as well as more complex ones to inspire and stretch those with previous experience. The projects also illustrate a diverse range of design approaches, demonstrating how different mosaic materials can be arranged and combined to create both abstract effects and representational images. The initial design of a piece is very important and should aim to make the most of all the interesting and unique possibilities of mosaic – color, texture, laying and grouting. The information and advice given in the projects on these subjects is also intended to help readers create successful designs for their own mosaic pieces. The different techniques described in the projects are clearly demonstrated with detailed advice about how to make a mosaic weatherproof and long lasting, and this technical information can also be applied to readers' own designs. There is also a comprehensive chapter at the front of the book that brings together all the vital information on materials, tools and techniques, providing an indispensable source of reference for all the practical aspects of making mosaics for the garden.

materials

Mosaic can be made of any material that comes in small pieces or that can be easily broken or cut, but garden mosaics must be able to withstand both the effects of water and extreme temperatures. Outdoor mosaics must therefore be made of hard materials such as stone, glass and ceramic which are impervious, frost proof and do not expand greatly when hot. These materials are all available in small sizes, which makes them easy to cut, and if properly fixed will produce durable and hardwearing surfaces.

Glass

Vitreous glass (1)
This is one of the most readily available mosaic materials and it offers a wide range of both subtle and bright colors.

The tiles are of a uniform size of 2 cm (¾ in) square by 4 mm (¼ in) thick and are manufactured in molds that give a flat face and a ridged back to provide a key for the adhesive. They are generally opaque and colored uniformly throughout and are also supplied on square paper-faced sheets of 15 tiles. There is a range of colors called "gem", which are shot through with a gold vein. Both ordinary and double-wheel tile nippers can be used for cutting, and care should always be taken when sweeping up the splinters as they can be sharp.

Stained glass (2)
Sheets of colored glass can be cut up to form mosaic pieces by cutting strips with a glasscutter and then nipping across with

tile nippers. They will be thinner than vitreous glass at 1 to 2 mm (¹⁄₁₆ to ¹⁄₁₂ in) thick and the appearance of translucent glass will be altered by the adhesive and backing material. It is therefore a particularly suitable material for translucent panels on glass backings and for sticking to mirrors using translucent adhesive.

Gold, silver and mirror (3)
Traditionally, gold and silver mosaics are made by laying metallic leaf over glass and then protecting the surface with a further layer of very thin glass. The backing glass is green and blue and these reverse faces have a depth and shine that can also be used very effectively. Slightly cheaper metallic tiles are also available with a clear glass face and a protective coat of varnish on the back, but these are

not so stable in outdoor conditions and may tarnish over time. Mirror tiles with plain and sandblasted finishes can also be used although the silvering will not last forever in exterior locations and may be affected by chemical reaction with cement-based adhesives. All these tiles can be cut with nippers although more accurate cuts may be achieved by scoring with a glasscutter first.

Smalti (4)

This is enameled glass made in a vast range of colors following a process developed in Roman times. A mixture of silica and potash or soda is heated with particular elements such as copper and lead according to special recipes that produce different colors. The mixture is poured out to form flat plates, like pizza bases, and cooled gradually. The plates are then usually cut up into 1.5 x 1 cm (½ x ⅜ in) rectangles which have uneven surfaces on the front and back faces. The material is remarkable for the intensity of the colors, making it highly suitable for architectural work over large areas seen from a great distance. The irregularity of the surface, however, makes it impractical in areas that must be kept clean, and the labor-intensive process of manufacture also makes it an expensive material to buy. Smalti can be cut with tile nippers, and the double-wheel nippers are particularly effective and reduce wastage.

Ceramic

Square unglazed ceramic (1, 2 & 3)

These tiles are manufactured in two sizes: 2 cm (¾ in) square **(1)** and 2.5 cm (1 in) square **(2)** and are available in a range of muted, earthy tones. They are identical on back and front faces, making them ideal for working in the indirect method and they also have crisp, square edges that lend themselves to cut-piece work. Tile nippers cut them easily although paler colors may be more likely to shatter. They

are available in random mixes of loose colors **(3)** or on paper-faced sheets. They can easily be soaked off the paper for cut-piece work or laid sheet by sheet for large plain areas. They are also available on mesh backing but this is not recommended for external locations.

Circular unglazed ceramic (4)

Made of the same material as the square tiles these little circles 2 cm (¾ in) diameter add variety to the ceramic range. They are also the same thickness as both the square ceramics and the vitreous glass so they can all be used together. Unfortunately the color range has dwindled recently and only two are currently available.

Broken china (5)

This is an increasingly popular source of mosaic material and readily available from garage sales and thrift shops. Newer china will be harder to cut but it will be very durable and frost proof. Objects that cut easily are fired at a low temperature and vulnerable to frosts, which may cause their glazed surface to chip away. If you are uncertain about the durability of your materials, bring the finished piece indoors over winter or protect it from frost with horticultural fleece. China can be smashed with a hammer and you should wear protective goggles and wrap the piece first in an old cloth so that fragments do not fly everywhere. More careful shaping can then be done with tile nippers.

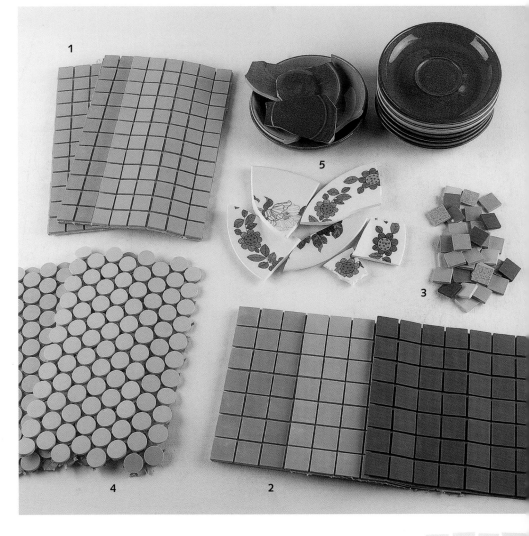

Marble, stone and pebbles

Marble rods (1)

This is a convenient form in which to buy marble. The rods are saw cut from polished tiles and are available in a variety of widths. They can be cut down into cubes with tile nippers or using the hammer and hardie.

Sheeted stone (2)

Some stone cubes are available in sheet form fixed to a mesh backing. They can be used for covering large areas or peeled individually off the mesh. Marble supplied on sheets will be as easy to cut with tile nippers as the loose cubes, but some colors will be much harder stones that are very difficult to cut by hand.

Pebbles (3)

Pebbles can be easily collected from beaches and rivers or bought in selected colors such as white, black and green.

They are also available in a wide range of sizes, from 1.5 cm (½ in) upwards. The white pebbles are soft and can be cut but are not suitable for areas of heavy wear.

Slate (4)

Slate can be found in garden centers in a range of beautiful colors but it is difficult to cut.

Marble cubes (5)

Marble tesserae can be cut to any size, although 1.5 cm (⅝ in) cubes are easy to work with and therefore most often used. They are cut down from 1 cm (⅜ in) thick polished marble tiles using a wet saw and have a polished face and a saw-cut face, either of which can be used. The polished face will have a high shine and a strong color with clear veins and markings. When used on floors, the grout joints between the small mosaic pieces will help to provide grip and prevent the surface from being too slippery. The unpolished

face will be much less intense in color and may have slight diagonal markings from the saw-blade. Tumbled cubes are also available which have been passed through a tumbling machine to soften the edges and dull the polished face to create a muted effect, half way between polished and unpolished. A similar effect is achieved by honing polished marble after it has been fixed. On large floors this is done with a machine but small pieces can be rubbed down with wet and dry abrasive paper.

It is also possible to split the cubes, revealing a rough inner face with a crystalline surface. This is called riven marble and can be used on wall mosaics. The textured effect is very lively and can be combined with the sympathetically uneven surfaces of smalti.

Marble can be cut with tile nippers, and long-handled nippers give greater leverage. The hammer and hardie can also be used to cut saw-cut rods down into cubes and to split and shape them.

Backing materials and fixing surfaces

Timber (1)

For exterior locations you must use an exterior grade board which can be either MDF (medium density fiberboard) or plywood (1). Because timber is a material that expands and contracts according to temperature and humidity a highly flexible adhesive such as BAL-Flex, or similar, is required. To reduce the amount of movement large boards should be braced at the back with battens of timber treated with preservative and screwed across the diagonals. The back of all timber boards should be protected from moisture with several coats of exterior paint or varnish.

Sand and cement slabs (2 & 3)

These are ideal surfaces to fix outdoor mosaic to, either in the form of cast paving slabs (2) or as in-situ coverings for walls or floors. The surface should be as flat as possible, as any irregularities will be visible in the surface of the mosaic. The sand and cement mixes should be completely dry before fixing the mosaic to prevent salts coming up through the joints, and exterior grade cement-based adhesives should be used. Paving slabs can be purchased either from garden centers or made in casting frames (3) which can be reused to create a series of slabs.

Tile-backer board (4)

This product has a foam core with a thin cement-based facing on either side. It is designed for lining domestic showers and bathrooms but makes a useful lightweight backing for mosaics. It can be glued directly to a wall surface with cement-based adhesive, or a timber batten treated with preservative can be glued to the back to allow screw fixing D-rings and wire hangers. On the ground it must be fully supported on a cement or sand bed as it has little strength and the applied loads must be transferred through to the ground below. The foam edge should be covered either with adhesive or a frame of either timber or metal angle as it deteriorates when exposed to light.

Timber and aluminium framing angle (5 & 6)

As well as creating a neat finish some kind of framing to a mosaic panel will help to protect the vulnerable edge pieces. Suitable materials for exterior use are hardwood and aluminium and a range of angles in a wide variety of sizes can be bought at hardware stores or timber merchants. You can cut them to fit your panel with a hacksaw, using a miter block or following a 45 degree angle drawn on the surface. Frames to timber boards can be screwed in place from the back, using galvanized steel or brass screws that will not rust, but tile-backer board can only be framed by sticking the angle to the back with silicone glue.

Ceramic floor tiles (7)

Floor tiles are fired at very high temperatures and can withstand outdoor conditions. They therefore make useful, relatively light, backings for small mosaic panels. They can be used on the ground, set into other paving or used as individual stepping stones, and can also be stuck to walls with tile adhesive if they are given some temporary support as the adhesive dries.

Terracotta and polystyrene

Terracotta can be used as a base for mosaics but in very cold areas these pieces, along with ordinary flowerpots, should be protected from frost in winter. The surface should be primed with dilute PVA glue before using cement-based adhesive for sticking. Polystyrene provides a stable base for outdoor mosaic but it is not very strong and would collapse if placed under any pressure or dropped. Again it should be primed with dilute PVA before sticking down with cement-based adhesive.

Other surfaces

Any rigid surface designed for outdoor use can be covered in mosaic but objects that bend, such as plastic furniture, are not suitable. The adhesive manufacturers should be consulted for specific requirements.

Adhesives and grouts

Cement-based adhesives

These are proprietary tiling adhesives based on traditional sand and cement but containing additives to improve adhesion and workability. Not all tiling adhesives are suitable for outdoor use so check the manufacturer's instructions carefully. Ready mixed products are available but powder-based products that are mixed with water give greater flexibility in consistency for different applications and will last indefinitely.

Latex/cement adhesives

These are two-part proprietary products, such as BAL-Flex, designed to give maximum flexibility and which combine a cement-based powder with a pure latex liquid. They are particularly suitable for bonding to timber bases that may suffer from expansion and warping due to changes in temperature and moisture content, especially in outdoor situations.

Epoxy

This is a two-part product that forms a genuinely waterproof setting bed. It is quite difficult to clean off the surface, particularly in mosaic where there are so many joints, and should be considered only when essential for reasons of hygiene or impermeability. It also creates a uniquely strong but flexible bond between a wide range of materials and may therefore be useful for exceptional repairs and restorations.

Cement-based grout

These are products that are a weak, sandy mix designed to fill the joints between the tiles while allowing some movement without cracking. Most are suitable for both indoor and outdoor use but always check individual manufacturer's instructions. They are generally available in a limited range of colors, including white, gray, ivory and black but some

manufacturers produce a full range of colors. Sometimes fine powder grouts are recommended for narrow joints but they can be difficult to clean off and the coarser, wide joint grouts are easier to use.

Wood glue

There is a type of wood glue that is yellow in color, described as aliphatic and marketed as Tite-Bond, that can be used in exterior locations. A waterproof version of PVA is available but it is waterproof only when used as an additive to, or in conjunction with, cement and should not be used as an exterior adhesive.

Silicone

Available in small tubes or cartridges for caulking guns, this glue is highly flexible and is suitable for both indoor and outdoor use. It comes in a translucent form, described as clear, which can be used on glass for translucent panels or for sticking glass to mirrors. Because it is very sticky and dries quickly it is important not to get it on the face of the tiles. It also forms an invisible skin after very short exposure to the air and so it should only be used to stick pieces one by one with the adhesive spread on the back of each tile.

Mirror adhesive

There are various proprietary mirror adhesives that are specially formulated for sticking both small and large mirrors to backing surfaces. They do not contain any solvents that might eat away at the silvering on the back and are also very flexible, allowing differential movement between the mirror and the backing.

tools

Most of the equipment you will need to make mosaic projects is readily available from DIY and craft shops. Many of the tools are exactly the same as those used for ordinary tiling, including the basic cutting tool, known as tile nippers or tile cutters. The double-wheel cutters and hammer and hardie are more specialist tools, as is the small notched trowel, and these are available from the suppliers listed at the back of the book.

Drawing equipment

Colored pencils (1)
Gather together a selection of colored pencils that match as closely as possible the range of mosaic colors with which you are working. The aim is to help design a successful mosaic rather than to produce a drawing that is beautiful in its own right but impossible to recreate in mosaic. Pastel pencils are particularly useful as colors can be mixed together to create better matches. They can also be easily erased which allows scope for revision and re-adjustment.

Geometry instruments (2)
Tools such as rulers, protractors, compasses and setsquares will help you set up geometric patterns as well as mark out the size of the brown paper you need to cut out if you are using the indirect method. The ruler and setsquare are also useful for gridding up the brown paper when you are enlarging your designs. A beam compass is useful for drawing large circles, although when drawing on paper you can improvise with a piece of string wound around a pencil and pulled taught from a drawing pin at the center.

Charcoal (3)
Charcoal is the ideal tool for sketching on to brown paper or other bases used in the direct method. It creates a bold and flowing line but can be erased and revised with ease. You can therefore make alterations even after you have started working and as the design develops through the process of making.

Paper (4)
Tracing paper is useful for both reversing designs and transferring them onto the rough side of brown paper if you are using the indirect method. It can also be used to transfer designs directly onto boards for the direct method.

Mosaic cutting tools

Heavy-duty tile nippers (1)
These tile nippers have extra long handles that give more leverage when cutting hard materials such as thick floor tiles and marble.

Tile nippers (2)
This is the essential tool for all mosaic cutting. The tungsten tipped blades can be used on all but the hardest mosaic materials for both cutting and shaping. They are bought with a spring attached but some people find them easier to use if the spring is removed. The back of the blades can be used as well as the front, which may be more convenient for some awkward cuts. The back will also stay sharp for longer and its use will extend the life of the nippers. Eventually the blades will become blunt and although it is not possible to sharpen them very well blunt nippers can be useful for cutting certain materials, such as some particular marble colors. However, other materials, such as gold and silver, will cut much better with a sharp pair of nippers.

Double-wheel nippers (3)
Double-wheel nippers are particularly good at cutting straight and accurate lines in vitreous glass and unglazed ceramic. Many people also use them for cutting smalti for greater accuracy and less wastage. They are designed so that the blades can be turned as they get blunt and it is a good idea to mark the point at which you start and always turn them the same way so that you use up the whole of the cutting edge in a methodical way. Replacement wheels are available.

Score and snap tile cutters (4)
These tools have a scoring wheel and a snapper for breaking the tiles. They are used when working with tiles larger than 2.5 cm (1 in) square to cut strips of the required size. These can then be cut across with nippers to form squares and rectangles. They can also be used on small tiles to cut triangles as the scoring encourages the tiles to break more neatly from point to point. The snapper is also useful when cutting glass. Larger versions are available with a fixed bed and a rail along which the scoring wheel runs, known as flat bed tile cutters.

Glass cutter (5)
These are sharp cutting wheels that score a line in the surface of glass sheets along which they will break when pressure is applied to either side. This can be done by gripping the glass between your thumb and fingers or using the snapper on the score and snap tile cutter.

Hammer and hardie (6)
The traditional method of cutting mosaic is to use a hammer and hardie. A mosaic hammer has a flat tungsten tip at each end, and a hardie is like a chisel embedded in a solid stand such as a tree trunk or a flowerpot filled with cement. The mosaic piece is held on top of the hardie along the line of the desired cut and the hammer brought down parallel to the hardie. You must avoid hitting the hammer blade itself on the hardie as this will blunt it or possibly break it.

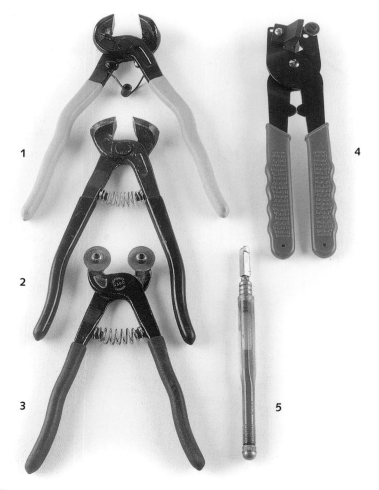

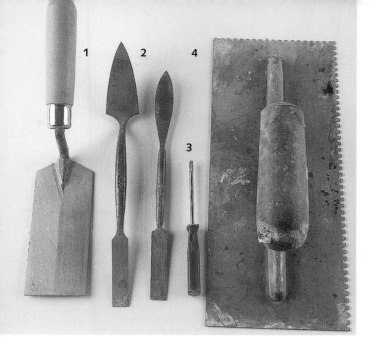
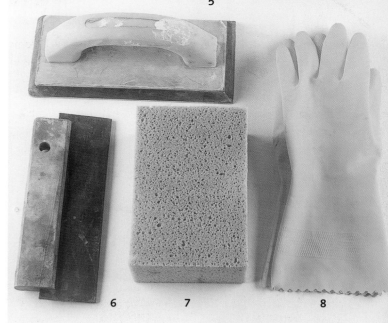

Mosaic fixing tools

Mixing trowel (1)
This angled trowel is very useful for mixing up grout and adhesive. It is also perfect for cleaning the sludge out of the bottom of buckets (this residue should always be thrown away rather than washed away as it plays havoc with the drains).

Putty knives/small trowel (2)
These little tools are perfect for applying adhesive to both curved and flat surfaces when using the indirect method. The pointed end can be maneuvered into the most awkward corners, and can also be used in the indirect method for spreading adhesive into areas that the larger trowel cannot easily reach.

Small screwdriver (3)
Although designed for other purposes, a little screwdriver is an indispensable tool for the mosaicist. It can be used to lever tiles off their backing, whether on paper or board, and to nudge them into alignment. It is also perfect for scraping adhesive out of joints and cleaning grout away from corners.

Small-notched trowel (4)
Small-notched trowels are used for applying cement-based adhesive for mosaic work. The small notches, about 3 mm (⅛ in) wide, ensure that most of the backing surface is covered in adhesive and even very small pieces of mosaic are in contact with the fixing bed. The notches mean that a very even bed of adhesive can be achieved, eliminating any thicker areas that would cause the adhesive to come up between the joints. The surface should be carefully examined for any thin areas of adhesive and a little extra can be added if too much has been scraped away. Be careful to clean the trowel before the adhesive dries, as it is hard work scraping it out of all the little notches.

Grouting tools

Grouting float (5)
This is a useful tool for grouting large areas of mosaic. Its sharp edge is particularly good at scraping away excess grout and helping to reduce wastage. It can also be used for pressing down on the mosaic face to flatten out any uneven areas and ensure a firm bond between the tiles and the adhesive bed.

Squeegee (6)
An alternative tool for grouting, the squeegee has a rubber blade that is used to spread the grout across the face of the mosaic. It can also be used to scrape away the excess grout and is more maneuverable in small areas than the float.

Tiler's sponge (7)
These sponges have a particularly close density that helps to pick up surplus grout and makes the job of cleaning the surface easier.

Rubber gloves (8)
The simplest way of spreading grout is by using your hands but you should always wear rubber gloves. The cement in the grout is very drying for the skin and some of the dark colors are also very staining. On three-dimensional objects there is no alternative method as floats and squeegees cannot cover curved surfaces with such accuracy and control.

Health and safety

Mosaic is a very low-tech craft and there are no power tools or heavy equipment involved. The opportunities for self-harm are therefore limited by taking a few simple precautions. Most important is to take some trouble in setting up your workstation. Mosaic is an engrossing activity and it is easy to find yourself working for hours in uncomfortable and awkward positions. You will be able to work for longer and with less discomfort if you make sure your working surface is at a convenient height, with a stool or chair that is compatible. When you find yourself having to stretch to reach particular areas think about turning the piece around so that it is closer to you or cutting the completed area off if you are following the indirect method. As with all manual work it is good practice to give yourself regular breaks when you can stretch and relax your muscles as well as taking the opportunity to stand back from your work and assess it from a greater distance. Listed below are a few pieces of equipment that will make your life easier and safer.

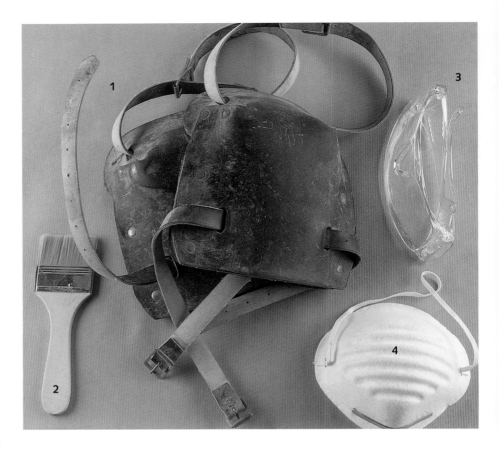

Knee pads (1)
If you are working on the ground it is a good idea to protect your knees with knee pads. These are available from building supply stores and hardware stores and can make life a lot more comfortable as well as protecting your joints from future problems. If you do not have knee pads you can place something soft on the floor instead, such as a cushion or some bubble-wrap.

Brushes (2)
Mosaic debris is often very sharp and it should always be cleared away with a brush rather than your hands. The pieces, however, are so small that the little cuts that you will inevitably get from time to time are never deep enough to cause lasting difficulty.

Protective goggles (3)
Cutting can also cause sharp splinters to fly off in unpredictable directions and goggles will protect your eyes from these shards. If you wear glasses these will do the same job, and you can get glasses with clear glass instead of lenses that are more comfortable to wear than goggles.

Masks (4)
All mosaic materials release dust when they are cut, and if you are cutting a large amount at one time, such as quartering glass or ceramic tiles, it is advisable to wear a facemask. Pouring powdered adhesives and grout can also create clouds of fine particles and a mask should be worn when mixing large quantities.

techniques

A wide range of techniques can be used in both the designing and fixing of mosaic projects. These are described in broad outline here and are also covered in more detail in the step-by-step projects. The method you choose for a project will depend on both its design and application, and choosing the right technique is vital for the success of the finished piece. Even if you are not making one of the designs in this book you will still be able to select the method most appropriate to your project and follow the detailed advice given.

Drawing

Drawing is not an essential skill for a mosaicist but it is useful to have a grasp of some basic techniques.

Color sketches

When you are designing your own mosaics it is very useful to sketch out your ideas before starting. Remember that the sketch is not an end in itself but simply provides a guide to the laying of the tiles. It can be much smaller than the finished piece but should be drawn in the same proportions and should take into account the size of the mosaic pieces when scaled down to the size of the drawing. You can cut bits out and try other solutions until you are happy with the idea. Of course, you do not have to follow the drawing exactly but it will help establish the overall balance of the piece and be a useful starting point.

Enlarging

To enlarge a sketch to the size of the mosaic it is easiest to work from a simple line drawing that can be made by tracing over a color original. A simple method is to draw a grid of squares over the line drawing and a grid of the same number of squares (but of a bigger size) on the backing surface of the mosaic. For the direct method this will be the backing board itself and for the indirect method it will be a piece of brown paper cut to size. The line drawing can then be copied, square by square, onto the larger surface. Charcoal is a good tool to use because it can be easily erased and adjusted. If you are using the indirect method you must remember to reverse the drawing at this stage by turning over the gridded tracing.

Tracing

For complex designs or where a great deal of precision is necessary it may be necessary to enlarge the design on a photocopier or scanner. The outlines can then be copied by hand onto tracing paper and the traced lines rubbed over with a soft pencil. This can be done on the back of the drawing if you are using the direct method, or the front of the drawing if you are reversing the image for the indirect method. The outline can then be drawn over again with a hard point (such as a ballpoint pen) on the opposite

Color sketches

Enlarging

side to the pencil rubbing so that the image is transferred onto the surface beneath, whether it is the backing board or the brown paper. Another way of transferring the image onto brown paper is to use a light box or to fix the original and the paper to a window. In either way the light will come through the opaque paper and allow the outlines of the original to be traced through onto the brown paper. Remember that to reverse the image it should face away from the brown paper.

Templates

There are small templates of the designs used in the projects at the back of this book (see pages 122–127). They can be enlarged using either of the techniques described above. There is an important relationship between the size of the individual mosaic pieces and the patterns they make so it is easiest to make the projects the same size that they are shown in the book. Some projects can be enlarged by using whole tiles instead of quarters, and it is always possible to add extra tiles around the edge to create a border and to fit a particular space. Template is also the term used to describe a piece of paper or wood used to establish the size and shape of a particular area. Brown paper can be laid down on the area you wish to mosaic and trimmed around the edges so that it makes a perfect fit, as if laying a carpet. The same paper can then be used to stick the tiles down on following the indirect method, but you must remember to stick to the back of the template so that the paper will be facing upwards when you come to fix the mosaic.

Cutting techniques

Vitreous glass and ceramic tiles are cut with tile nippers by placing the nippers at the edge of the tile and squeezing gently. The angle at which the nippers are placed will determine the angle of the cut. Tiles can also be nibbled away to form circles or to straighten up uneven cuts. Remember that cuts do not have to be perfectly straight – some variety of shape and size will give the mosaic its hand-made quality. Marble is easier to cut if the nippers are placed across the tile rather than at the edge. Marble and stone mosaic can be cut using the hammer and hardie. When striking the stone with the hammer try to avoid hitting the hardie underneath as this will blunt it or even break the blade.

Cutting circles and other curves

These shapes can be cut by nibbling the corners off a square tile with tile nippers. If the edge is too jagged you can keep nibbling away these small points until a smooth line is achieved.

Cutting triangles

These are most easily cut using score and snap tile cutters. Score a line from corner to corner and place the snapper at right angles to the score line. Squeeze gently and the tile should cut neatly along the score line. If there is a small nib protruding on one side this can be easily removed with tile nippers.

Cutting strips

Long, narrow strips are best cut with double-wheel cutters, which should be positioned in the middle of the tile rather than at the edge. Start by cutting the tile in half and then cut each half again.

Cutting circles

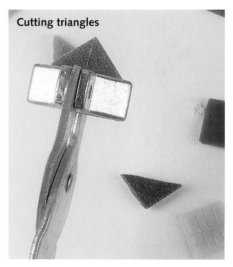

Cutting triangles

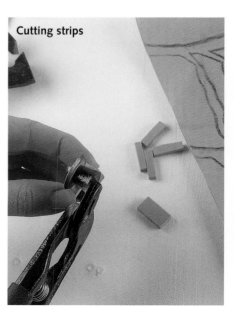

Cutting strips

Laying techniques

The character of a mosaic is determined by the way in which the individual pieces are laid. Different degrees of regularity and dynamism can be used to create different effects of movement and stillness, animation and calm.

Spacing

The width of joints between tiles is largely a matter of personal preference. They can be butted up together and the piece left ungrouted or they can be spaced as much as 4 or 5 mm (¼ in) apart. A general rule is that whatever spacing you choose you should aim to follow throughout the piece so that it has an overall consistency. Larger mosaics on walls and floors (over 50 cm/20 in square) should have a minimum joint width of at least 1 mm (¹⁄₁₆ in) to allow for expansion and contraction.

Lines of laying

Because mosaic is made up of tiny pieces the way in which they relate to each other provides a unique set of opportunities and visual effects. If you are converting an image from another medium the most challenging decisions will be about how to lay the tiles so that the pattern created by the grout joints is in sympathy with the rest of the design. Equally, if you are designing a mosaic, these patterns are an essential and enlivening part of your vocabulary and can be used as designs in themselves as well as complementing other components such as color and shape.

The simplest way of laying tiles is to follow lines, either in rows, known as *Opus Tessalatum* or in curves, known as *Opus Vermiculatum*. The lines can be generated by the outlines of the objects

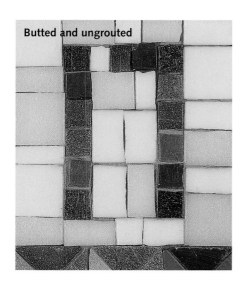
Butted and ungrouted

Opus Tessalatum

Widely spaced

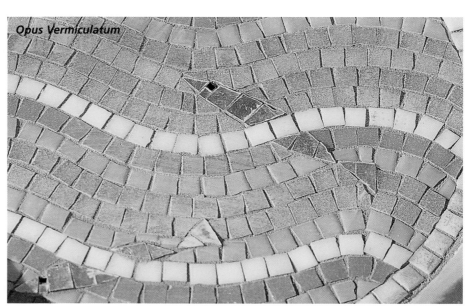
Opus Vermiculatum

Opus Regulatum

Opus Palladianum

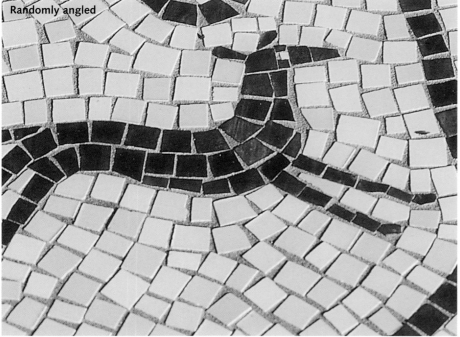

Randomly angled

depicted or they can be chosen to give a sense of direction or movement. Undulating lines are often used to create the impression of the movement of water and this dynamic use of lines of laying is known as "andamenti."

The other way of laying tiles is to cover a surface with an overall pattern that does not create any particular sense of direction. One such method is to lay the tiles to a grid, known as *Opus Regulatum*, and you can sometimes use sheeted up tiles as supplied by the manufacturer. This may appear to be the simplest of all techniques but the fierce regularity of the grid can result in some very awkward cuts and tiny pieces when cutting into motifs. Outlining the motifs in the background color before cutting in can help to disguise these difficulties.

Another non-directional method is known as *Opus Palladianum* and is made up of randomly cut halves and triangles laid to interlock like crazy paving. This is a quick way of filling in complex background shapes and creating a surface that is lively but not dominating. A variant is to use squares, quarters and halves mixed together and laid perpendicular to each other but not creating rows in any one direction.

A final method using square tiles is to lay them at randomly tilted angles creating large and irregular shaped grout joints and a flickering mosaic surface. The size of the joints will tone down the intensity of the mosaic color but this can sometimes be used to advantage and with strong colors, such as white, black or gold, the effect is not significant.

materials, tools and techniques

Fixing

The techniques of fixing mosaic are closely related to tiling techniques. If you are embarking on a big project it is a good idea to make a small sample first to enable you to become familiar with the fixing process and also to check that the mosaic will look as you wish when it is grouted and finished. The techniques are illustrated in step-by-step detail in the various projects. This section gives a broad outline of the methods and a guide to choosing the right technique for different applications.

The direct method

This method of fixing is when the tiles are glued directly to the backing surface. The adhesive used can be cement-based, wood glue or silicone depending on the particular application, and it is a method that is suitable for all mosaic and backing materials. It is an appealing method because you can get an immediate idea of the finished appearance of the piece as you work. It is also a suitable technique for working with materials, such as glazed tiles, that have a different color and appearance on the back. You can also work in this way with materials of varying thickness, building up the thinner pieces with extra cement-based adhesive if a flatter surface is desired. Once all the pieces are stuck down the piece is grouted and sponged clean.

One of the limitations of the method is that it is difficult to achieve a perfectly flat surface and is therefore not suitable for floors. It is also difficult to make changes and amendments once the pieces are stuck down, and designs therefore must be worked out in detail in advance or follow a strict system. A further difficulty is found when working with cement-based adhesives because they are thick and opaque and therefore obliterate any underlying drawing. There are also sometimes practical disadvantages of working in-situ if it involves high walls or prolonged kneeling on cold patio floors, and for outdoor mosaics you can only work when the weather is good.

Direct onto three-dimensional forms

The direct method is the only practical way of covering complex curved surfaces. Cement-based adhesive should be used because it will hold the tiles immediately onto vertical and sloping surfaces. Terracotta and other porous surfaces should be sealed with a 50:50 mix of PVA glue with water to prevent the adhesive drying out too fast.

Direct method

Direct onto three-dimensional forms

The indirect method

This technique, sometimes called the reverse method, is when the design is reversed and drawn onto brown paper and the pieces stuck upside down with water-soluble glue. It sounds complicated but it is a method that has many advantages. The drawing on the paper can still be seen through the thin layer of glue and the design can be followed with accuracy. Also, any alterations can be made easily while the mosaic is still on the paper by damping the back and removing the offending pieces. The work can be carried out comfortably on a bench or table even if it is destined for a ceiling, floor or vertical wall panel. Larger pieces can also be undertaken and cut up into smaller sections with a sharp blade along convenient lines in the design as the work progresses. These sections (usually about 50 cm/20 in square and larger) can then be transported to their final location.

The fixing process must be carried out as a continuous sequence and breaks only taken when the mosaic sections have been peeled and cleaned. For large mosaics this does not mean fixing every section, but simply never leaving any particular section half fixed.

The fixing process starts by applying a coat of grout to the back of the mosaic, which is called pre-grouting. The backs of the tiles should be sponged clean, leaving the grout in the joints to prevent any adhesive coming through. In this state, the mosaic is fragile and the sections should be fixed immediately to the backing surface. A bed of cement-based adhesive should be applied with a small-notched trowel, covering an area of three or four sections at a time. Once the sections have been firmly pressed into the adhesive, the paper facing can be dampened and the water-soluble glue allowed to dissolve. After about 15 minutes the paper can be peeled off carefully and the surface of the mosaic sponged down. This will spread excess grout across the face of the tiles but it will also smooth down the grout in the joints and create a better finish in the end. Repeated sponging with the clean face of a sponge will remove the surface grout and the mosaic can be left to dry. A final grout will be necessary to fill any holes and the joints between the sections and then the mosaic can be sponged down and polished with a dry cloth.

The indirect method cannot be used easily when there are extreme differences of thickness in the mosaic materials, although the uneven surface of smalti can be fixed by applying a thin layer of adhesive to the back of the mosaic instead of grout, sometimes called buttering the back. Surfaces that curve in one direction, such as cylindrical columns or barrel vaults, can easily be covered using the indirect method but more complex surfaces, such as domes or sculptures, are much more difficult.

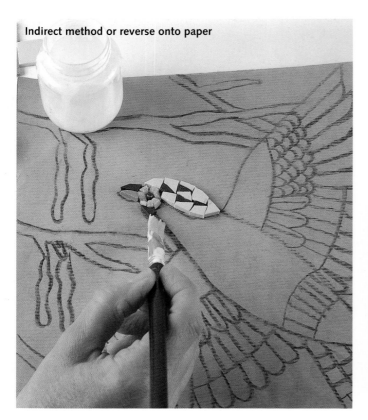

Indirect method or reverse onto paper

Buttering the back

Casting

This is a method of making slabs and pavers for outdoor use. The mosaic is stuck down to paper with water-soluble glue and then placed in the bottom of a casting tray. This is a wooden box with removable sides and which should be coated on the base and sides with petroleum jelly so that the slab does not stick to it. The mosaic should be grouted from the back with a creamy mixture of cement and water and the residue should be scraped off with a trowel. The tray should then be filled half way up with a mix of one part cement to three of sand and enough water to make a thick paste. For larger slabs, a piece of stainless steel mesh should then be laid in the tray to act as reinforcement and then fill the tray with more of the sand/cement mixture. The tray should then be wrapped in plastic and left to cure for up to one week, depending on the nature of the project. It will not have achieved its full strength so the operation should be handled with care, and a board placed over the back of the slab to support it when it is turned over. The paper can be dampened and carefully peeled back. Then the surface can be regrouted with the cement slurry and sponged clean. The slab should then be rewrapped and left for a further two weeks before using.

This technique produces a very flat surface and is useful when using mosaic materials of different thicknesses. However, it is a slow process and the resulting slabs are very heavy and anything larger than 30 cm (12 in) square can be difficult to handle. An easier way of producing a mosaic paving slab is to buy a precast concrete slab from a garden center and then apply a mosaic to the surface using the indirect method. It is also possible to cast a plain slab and fix the mosaic to it afterwards, using the direct method. This allows you to make a slab to whatever size or shape you need and is described in detail in the cast slab project on pages 70–75.

Grouting

Grouting is the process of filling the joints between the individual pieces with a weak mixture of sand and cement, described as grout. Purely decorative mosaics do not necessarily have to be grouted; in small pieces tiles can be butt-jointed so that the backing material cannot be seen, or the adhesive bed can be left visible behind the joints. The absence of grout can intensify the colors and also give the piece a more textured surface. Mosaics in locations that need to be cleaned, such as floors, splashbacks and table tops, will need to be grouted in order to create a uniform surface.

Pre-grouting

This process is an essential part of the indirect method (see page 22). Grout is applied with any of the tools described on page 15 to the back of the paper-faced mosaic. The backs of the tiles are sponged clean, leaving the grout to fill the joints.

Casting a slab

Pre-grouting

This stops the adhesive from coming up between the joints and improves the adhesion of the mosaic to the backing material. It also begins to dampen the water-soluble glue, making the paper easier to remove but also makes the mosaic more vulnerable at this stage. It will hold together for at least 10 or 15 minutes but it is important not to leave it too long or the tiles will start to drop off when you turn the piece over into the adhesive bed. When the paper has been peeled away the excess grout on the face of the mosaic must be sponged off while it is still wet or it will harden into an uneven surface.

Grouting

In the direct method grout is applied in a single process when the adhesive is completely dry. The entire surface of the mosaic is covered in the wet grout mixture, which should have the consistency of a thick paste, using any of the tools described on page 15. The grout should be pressed down so that it fills all the joints and then the excess on the surface of the tiles should be scraped

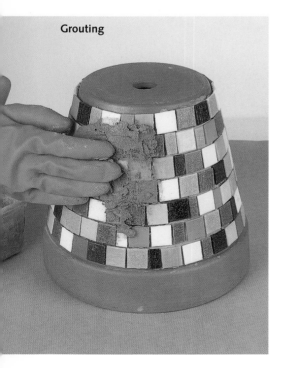

Grouting

off as much as possible. Finally, the surface should be sponged clean with a tiler's sponge. The sponge should be squeezed out so that it is damp rather than wet, and you should only ever pass a clean face of the sponge across the face of the mosaic. Turning the sponge and rinsing it regularly will prevent the grout from being spread back across the surface. Try not to go over the mosaic too often with the sponge as each pass will take more grout out of the joints. Any slight residue of grout on the surface can be wiped off with a dry rag while the grout is still slightly damp (after about 30 minutes).

Regrouting

The technique for regrouting a mosaic made in the indirect method is exactly the same as described above for grouting mosaics made with the direct method. Dampening the surface with a sponge first will make it easier to spread the grout. Any mosaic can be grouted again if there are small holes and cracks that need to be filled. If you are unhappy with the grout color regrouting in a different color tends to produce a very patchy result. Applying mortar cleaner to the surface will eat away at the grout a little bit leaving more room for the new color. Cleaning off the new color should be done with great care as you will easily wash the grout away but on smaller pieces the process is definitely possible. Another way of darkening the grout color and recreating the effect of wet grout is to oil the mosaic with linseed oil. This will sink into the joints and can be washed off the surface of the tiles with a mild detergent after about 15 minutes.

Buffing up

As the grout dries a dusty film may begin to appear across the surface of the mosaic. This can be rubbed off with a clean, dry cloth, preferably before the grout is completely dry.

Finishing and hanging

Framing

The edges of mosaics are always vulnerable to accidental damage, and pieces that are going to be handled or knocked, such as tabletops, should have a protective edging. If possible they should be fixed onto a board that is already framed. Timber frames should be painted before fixing the mosaic and protected with masking tape. If necessary, aluminium or hardwood angle can be added after the mosaic is finished, taking great care not to damage the mosaic. It can either screwed into a timber backing board or glued with silicone glue.

Framing – painted hardwood

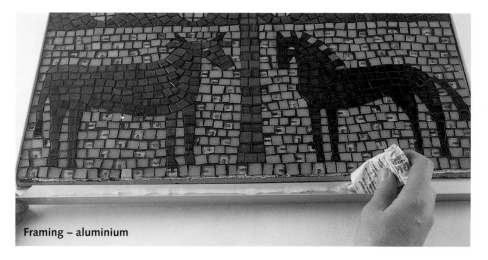

Framing – aluminium

Edging

The edges of unframed pieces can be strengthened by running a little extra adhesive around the sides. This also disguises the foam core of tile-backer board and gives the appearance of a cement slab. Although it leaves an uneven surface it can be painted a different color if desired when the adhesive is dry. Mosaics can also be edged with copper strip pinned into the edge of the board with copper tacks.

Fixings

Heavy panels can be hung from the wall using a pair of L-shaped or angled battens. One is screwed securely to the wall and the inverse to the back of the panel. The two battens interlock, creating an invisible but secure fixing. Alternatively, the board can be screwed directly to the wall behind through holes where the mosaic pieces have been left off. This allows fixings to be made across the whole area of the panel, which prevents it warping and bowing. The mosaic tiles can then be stuck over the screw heads and grouted in to create an invisible fixing. It is a good idea to take a photograph of the mosaic before covering the fixing holes to record their position in case you need to remove the piece at a later date. Pieces on tiles or tile-backer board can be glued to walls with a thin layer of cement-based adhesive. Some temporary support, such as a timber batten, may be required to take the weight of the mosaic while the adhesive dries.

Edging

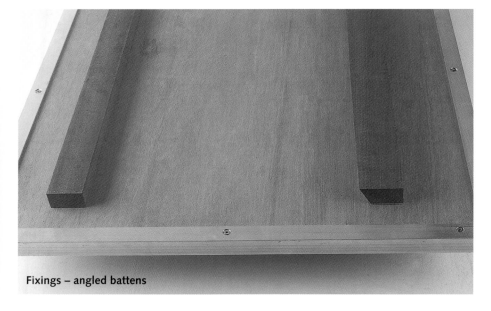

Fixings – angled battens

projects

table top
page 32

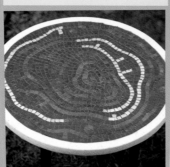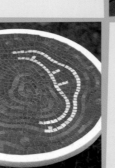

**flying jay
wall plaque**
page 76

seat
page 80

runner bean
page 84

wall panel
page 90

china plant pot
page 100

**two beasts
under a tree**
page 94

cast fossil paver
page 108

sphere
page 104

blue cat
page 112

slate paver
page 118

house number

This is always a popular project for beginners as it is a small piece but also has an immediate practical purpose. It can be adapted for any number and the overall size adjusted for longer and shorter ones. The design has a pleasing simplicity that demonstrates how highly decorative effects can be achieved simply by the careful selection of colors. It depends on an illusion of three dimensions created on a flat surface by the arrangement of triangles of different tones of the same color. The two opposite dark faces alternating with light and mid-tones suggest the form of a pyramid and the illusion is intensified because the piece is not grouted and the tiles directly abut each other. The colors chosen are mostly slightly murky rather than bright primaries, but carefully disposed on each side is one combination, such as the yellows or reds, that has greater intensity than the rest. The background to the numbers is filled with two shades of white to add some further visual interest, and the numbers themselves are made up of the darkest colors in the border. The high contrast between the figures and the background makes the house number clear and legible which is an important practical consideration!

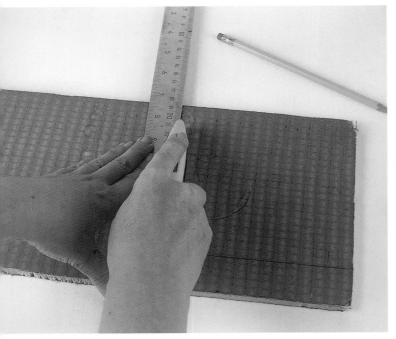

1 Select the shape of your plaque from the three templates on page 122, then measure and mark out the appropriate size on the tile-backer board with a pencil. Cut out the square or rectangle with a sharp hobby knife using a metal straight edge as a guide. The blade will cut through the top layer and the foam first. A second cut will be needed to penetrate the bottom layer.

2 Select the groups of colors needed to create the "pyramid" border pattern. You will need a dark, light and mid-tone of each color and will use two dark triangles and one of each of the others to make each pyramid. Cut the square vitreous glass tiles in half across the diagonal. Using a score and snap cutter, score with the wheel a line from corner to corner.

3 Place the tile under the snapper so that the score line is parallel to the handles and at 90 degrees to the snapper. Squeeze gently and the tile should break neatly along the score line. Sometimes one of the corners will be left with a protruding nib which can easily be nibbled away with tile nippers.

4 When you have cut the triangles you are ready to start sticking the border. Apply a band of cement-based adhesive the width of the border along the side of the board and carefully place the tiles in sequence. Push them tightly together so that there are no gaps in between.

5 Before sticking down the numbers, lay a row of whole and half white tiles down each side and half tiles at the top and bottom. This will help you lay the numbers straight and also minimize cutting. The figures can then be laid using quarter tiles and finally the gaps between filled in with white tiles cut to fit.

6 The edges of the mosaic will be vulnerable to knocking and can be reinforced by running some extra adhesive around the side of the panel. This also covers up the exposed edge of the foam core which must be protected from direct light (foam crumbles when exposed to ultra violet light). The finished piece will be very lightweight and can be stuck to the wall using cement-based tile adhesive as though it were a wall tile. This will be a permanent fixing but you are unlikely to want to take your house number with you when you move.

tools and materials

Circular plywood table with a hardwood base and legs

Brown paper, cut to size

Water-soluble glue

Pencil

Tile nippers

Ceramic tiles

Vitreous glass tiles

Masking tape

BAL-Flex, or two-part latex adhesive suitable for use outside

Flat-bed squeegee

3 mm (1/8 in) notched trowel

Sponge

Bucket for water

Rubber gloves

table top

This small garden table is made using a combination of glass and unglazed ceramic. Although the tiles are cut in irregular shapes, the grout lines run through, matching the variation of size as they broaden and narrow in width. This helps produce a sense of naturalism, appropriate in an exterior context. The design develops from center to edge, following the logic of an increasingly irregular circular form, combining predictability of cut with a naturalistic uneven quality – rather reminiscent of a slice through the trunk of a tree. Irregularity is nothing to fear. Beginners sometimes feel that every tile should be drawn onto the paper, every curve made with a compass, every line drawn with a ruler. This is not strictly necessary as a pleasantly controlled irregularity is often far more charming. It is worth pointing out the importance of finishing off the piece with the right frame. Originally a gray color was chosen to frame the piece, but eventually it was decided that a lighter tone worked more effectively with the line of pale blue vitreous glass and the frame was repainted. The juxtaposition of materials – unglazed ceramic next to vitreous glass – introduces a note of freshness: a contrast that complements both.

1 A number of unglazed ceramic tiles in soft hues of brown and blue have been chosen for this project. Both colors are muted in nature so the introduction of the vitreous glass produces a pleasing contrast. The lavender blue is particularly vibrant against the browns, so it will be placed so it adjoins them.

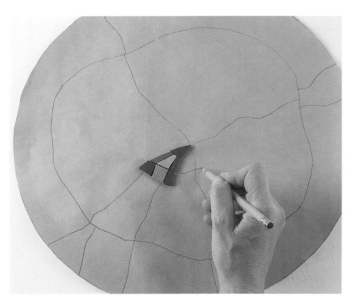

2 The center of the design is the place from which all the lines radiate, so it is important to start cutting and laying from here. The design does not need to be sketched out in its entirety onto the paper, but it can be helpful to draw one or two guidelines to follow. As the lines radiate outwards and the glass ring contorts in shape, it is sometimes necessary to cut two tiles to make a single one (see Step 5). This can be done in a vertical, as well as a horizontal, axis.

3 With a design like this, which depends on accurate cutting, sketching the required cuts on to the tile is of invaluable assistance. Do this with a pencil.

4 Once the required shape has been marked onto the tile, simply cut along the line with the tile nippers.

5 To move from a broader to a narrower shape in an elegant fashion, simply make flat-ended cuts as they meet the adjacent tile, as shown in the picture. A flat-ended cut is a more subtle way of decreasing or increasing the width of a line than a triangular cut is. A couple of vitreous glass tiles have been laid in the center to connect the bright outer band to the point from which all the rings radiate.

6 The mosaic being complete, it is time to decide on the color of the frame. This dark gray seemed too somber, so a lighter tone was used.

7 During the fixing process, it is essential to mask the frame, to protect the newly painted wood. It can be helpful to use the table base to hold the unfixed mosaic as it is pre-grouted. Using the flat-bed squeegee, push the grout into the joints with the rubbery end of the tool. Scrape away the excess grout in the same way. When you have finished, rinse the squeegee in a bucket of water.

8 When the entire mosaic has been grouted and the surplus removed with the squeegee, sponge off any traces that remain. Use each side of the sponge only once. Dabbing with the sponge simply puts back grout that has already been removed. When all the sides of the sponge have been used, rinse it out in a bucket of clean water and repeat the operation until the mosaic is clean. Remove the mosaic from the table base and set aside.

9 Apply the cement-based adhesive across the whole of the base of the recessed area with the notched trowel. The tiles will not stick to any spot not entirely covered with adhesive so it pays to be thorough. Once the adhesive is evenly distributed, pick up the pre-grouted mosaic, turn it over, and carefully place it, paper-side-up, into the recess. Take the clean flat-bed squeegee and tap the mosaic into place, ensuring proper contact with the adhesive throughout.

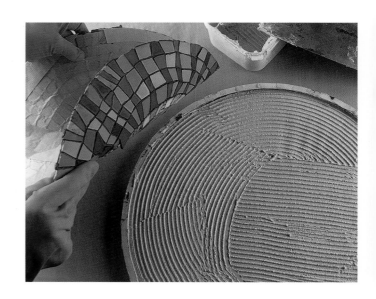

table top

10 Wet the sponge and gently squeeze out excess water. Wet the paper thoroughly and leave it to absorb the moisture. This may take about 10 minutes. If the paper starts to dry out during this period, re-wet with the sponge. When the paper has darkened in color and has clearly absorbed the moisture, peel it off, starting from one side. The recess helps to hold the mosaic into position so the paper can be peeled off in a single piece from one side only.

11 When all the paper has been removed, clean the mosaic gently with a damp but thoroughly squeezed-out sponge and leave until the adhesive has cured. This generally takes about 24 hours. When the adhesive is dry, regrout carefully from the front. Sponge the surface clean. Once the grout is dry, remove the masking tape. Buff up the surface with a dry cloth. The table can now be placed on its legs and into the garden.

23 cm (9 in) diameter
terracotta flowerpot

Vitreous glass tiles

PVA glue

Large paintbrush

Tile nippers

Grey cement-based
adhesive

Putty knife or small trowel

Gray grout

Rubber gloves

Tiler's sponge

simple flower pot

This striking pot is easy to make and a lot more stylish than a plain terracotta pot. It is covered in a random mix of vitreous glass tiles, but the colors have been chosen with great care to create an effect that is both subtle and lively. Mixing colors together in this way is great fun and there are lots of different effects you can achieve. Calm mixes can be made by using colors of the same tone together so that they almost blend but also create a slight flickering effect that is much more interesting than a single color would be. This is often a useful approach for background colors but on its own it can be enlivened with occasional flashes of brighter color. The mix chosen for this project uses colors of all tones, from white to very dark brown, and also some bright highlight colors. With such a variety of ingredients a completely random approach could result in a chaotic mess and a careful balance has to be achieved between the visual interest of the unexpected juxtapositions and an overall effect that maintains some cohesion. The eye is naturally attracted by variety, but it is also unsettled by uneven and haphazard groupings which have no pattern or rhythm. In practice this means that you have to think about the positioning of every tile in relation to the colors around it and because mosaics are applied one by one, it is one of the advantages of the medium that this degree of control is easy and pleasurable to achieve. Laying the random mix is not a simple mechanical task but one that engages the eye at every step.

1 Make a careful selection of tiles, taking account of their relative light and darkness as well as their color. In this project there is a very dark brown tile and a white tile, and in between these extremes there are four graduated mid tones of blue and purple. In addition there are three brighter colors, two oranges and a pink, which give livelier accents to the mix.

2 Prime the pot with a 20:80 PVA to water mix to reduce the absorbency of the pot and stop the adhesive drying out too quickly.

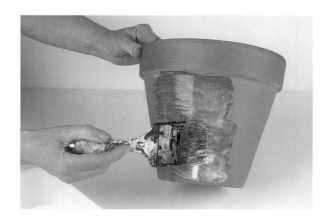

3 To avoid knocking tiles off as you work, it is a good idea to turn the pot over so that the rim is resting on the table. Start sticking the first row above the rim by placing a little dab of adhesive on the back of each tile with a putty knife or small trowel and then placing it carefully on the surface of the pot. Every now and then you should introduce a cut tile so that when they are absolutely necessary – for instance at the end of a row – they will not stand out as an ugly oddity.

simple flower pot

4 To avoid turning the pot all the time, work vertically upwards, one section at a time. Choose each color with care so that they are all regularly dispersed across the surface. Try to avoid the vertical joints lining through by staggering the tiles and adding cut tiles when the joints begin to coincide.

5 Continue around the pot, turning it as you complete each section. When you come to the final section there will be cuts required to finish off each row so remember to try to disperse them across the width of the section. If they are all on top of each other it will interrupt the regularity of the arrangement and stand out in an awkward way.

6 When the tiles are all stuck down and the adhesive is dry, usually in about twelve hours depending on the air temperature and humidity, the piece can be grouted. Mix the gray grout to a thick paste with water and apply with your hands protected in rubber gloves. Work the grout into the joints and scrape off the excess with the side of your hand.

7 Finally, sponge the surface clean with a damp sponge. Always wipe with a clean face of the sponge so as not to spread the grout back over the face of the tiles. As the piece dries, but before it is completely dry, rub off any residual grout with a clean, dry cloth.

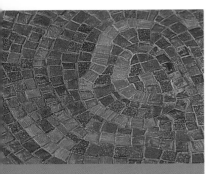

tools and materials

Terrazzo table base

Brown paper, cut to size

Washable PVA glue

Side-tile nippers

Wheeled cutters (for use with gold and copper)

Masking tape

3 mm (⅛ in) notched trowel

Flat-bed squeegee

Sponge

Bucket of water

Containers for mixing grout and adhesive

Anthracite colored grout

Cement-based adhesive

Rubber gloves

Gold and copper tiles

Vitreous glass tiles

terrazzo table

Although this design may look complicated, it is in fact very simple to make. Of all mosaic materials, vitreous glass is the most forgiving of elementary cutting skills. The design is based on color contrast, so if another palette seemed preferable it could be substituted without difficulty. The base onto which this mosaic is laid is terrazzo, an ideal substrate for use outside. Mosaic and terrazzo are traditional Italian crafts. They have a number of materials in common – marble chippings, lime, cement and stone dust. Terrazzo professionals are often adept at both crafts, and it is not unusual to see them combined. The practicality of terrazzo makes it ideal for use in the garden. It can be an attractive substitute for sand and cement, another equally practical material. The design does not depend on having the base made in terrazzo – it could be fixed to almost any surface. One of the most troublesome aspects of mosaic making outside is finding a substrate that can withstand a wide range of temperatures and is not sensitive to water. It is important, as we stress elsewhere, to protect surfaces from the ravages of the elements. Providing you follow the technical guidance given in the book, most of these designs could be fixed in a number of ways.

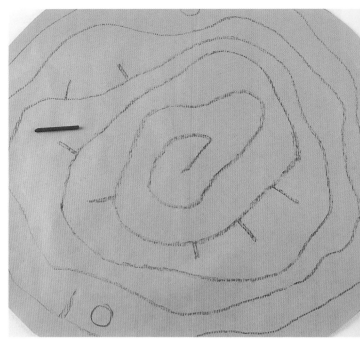

1 This terrazzo base is an ideal depth for vitreous mosaic. Just enough room has been allowed for the thickness of the mosaic tile and the adhesive to hold it in place, so when the mosaic is fixed, it will be flush with the terrazzo rim. It is important to ensure the mosaic is laid flush, or water might pool on the table. Cut out a piece of brown paper that fits neatly into the recess. A number of purple mauve tiles have been chosen as a background, along with three varieties of red, which will be used for the line.

2 This design is really just a simple spiral, but an unvarying spiral relentlessly circling to the center of the table can have rather a pedestrian appearance. This more freestyle idea is no trickier to execute, but the meandering line is less predictable and gives a certain organic quality to the design. Using charcoal, draw a line onto the rough rather than the polished side of the paper.

3 The red line is structured by tone, mostly dark, building here and there to occasional outbreaks of more brilliant color. It can be helpful to create a key plotting the gradation of tones from dark to light. It is surprisingly easy to misidentify a color when faced with a heap of closely similar ones. The key can be used to help match a brighter or more muted tile. The background is laid in an entirely haphazard way. So too, are the copper and gold.

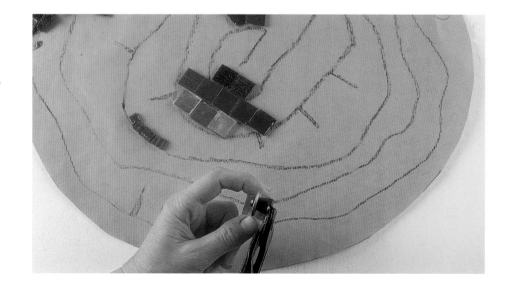

4 Begin laying the tiles, gluing them to the paper with a 20:80 solution of washable PVA and water. Always start with the most important feature in any mosaic design – in this case the red line. Place the nippers precisely centrally on the edge of the glass tile, and squeeze gently. Do not worry if the tiles are not all perfect quarters, a certain irregularity adds character to the design. Because the reverse method is being used here, stick down the side of the tiles you ultimately wish to see; so if you want the table to be flat, the tiles need to be laid ridged side upwards. It might seem sensible to lay the whole of the red line first, before embarking on the purple background, but laying and sticking both areas at the same time, as shown here, means you can amend the position of the line in accordance with what you cut.

5 Tile nippers are very useful for most mosaic tasks, but there are one or two jobs that are made considerably easier by using other tools. The wheeled cutters used here make the job of cutting gold, silver and metallic glass tiles considerably easier. Tiles made with precious metals are expensive, so it is worth having an accurate tool. These gold tiles show their gold on the back as well as the front, but the copper ones have a protective laminate making them look rust brown. Continue cutting and laying the tiles until the piece is complete. Set the piece aside until the glue is dry and prepare the materials for the process of fixing the mosaic.

Tiles can be levered from the paper quite easily with a small screwdriver – the kind used for electrical plugs. If you happen to create a hole in the paper, simply patch it up with a small piece of brown paper. You do not need to glue it into place – the glue with which you stick the replacement tile will do the trick.

6 Mask the edge of the terrazzo table. This can be done neatly and accurately if small strips of masking tape are cut, as they allow for the curve of the rim. If left unmasked the grout may stain the terrazzo.

7 Take the mosaic, now stuck to the sheet of paper, and place it within the table's recess. This helps to hold the mosaic in place as you grout. A flat-bed squeegee is a very good tool when all the materials are the same thickness. Push the grout into the joints with the rubbery flat end of the tool and when this has been done, remove the excess grout in the same way.

8 When the entire mosaic has been grouted, sponge off the excess. Wet the sponge and squeeze it out until it is as dry as possible. With a slightly curving motion, run the full face of the sponge across the table, to maximize the surface area. Use each side of the sponge only once and rinse thoroughly before sponging the surface clean again.

9 Apply the cement-based adhesive to the recessed area using the notched trowel. The tiles will not stick to any spot not entirely covered with adhesive so it pays to be thorough. Once the adhesive is evenly distributed, pick up the pre-grouted mosaic, turn it over and carefully place, paper-side-up, into the recess. Take the clean flat-bed squeegee and tap the mosaic into place, ensuring proper contact with the adhesive throughout.

10 Wet the sponge but do not squeeze it out to the same extent as before. Wet the paper thoroughly and leave it to absorb the moisture. When the paper has changed from a light to a dark color and has clearly absorbed the moisture, peel it off carefully, starting from one side. When all the paper has been removed, clean the mosaic gently with a damp but thoroughly sqeezed-out sponge, and leave until the adhesive has cured. This generally takes about 24 hours.

11 When the adhesive is dry, regrout carefully from the front. Sponge the surface clean. Once the grout is dry, remove the masking tape. Buff up the surface with a dry cloth. The table can now be placed on its legs and into the garden.

35 cm (14 in) outside diameter terracotta saucer

Vitreous glass mosaic tiles

Silver tiles

Brown paper

Charcoal

Small brush

Washable PVA glue

Scissors

Tile nippers

Double-wheel tile cutters

Gray grout

Gray cement-based adhesive

Rubber gloves

Tiler's sponge

Notched adhesive trowel

Silver spray paint

bird bath

This project is quite easy to make and its simplicity is essential to the elegance of its design. It uses the indirect method of sticking to paper first (see techniques on page 22) and is a good introduction to this useful technique. The design is based on the way that water is often described in traditional mosaics, using parallel waving lines to create an attractive rhythmical pattern evoking the undulating surface of water and its flowing movement. The colors chosen are pale, watery greens and grays, with only a little of the more obvious pale blue, and this gives the piece a subtle, shimmering quality. This is enlivened by the little flashes of silver used to make the small fish swimming amongst the waves. An important feature of the design is the use of white, which stands out brightly and defines both the circle and the structure of the waves. White is also used to run in front of the little fish to create the stylised illusion that they are within the water and not leaping over it. The finishing touch is to spray the terracotta dish with silver paint so that the surrounding saucer harmonizes with the delicate colors of the mosaic.

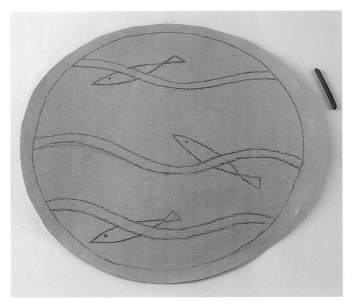

1 Terracotta saucers are readily available as bases to flower pots. Before starting the mosaic, seal the terracotta with a 20:80 solution of PVA and water. This makes the terracotta less absorbent and prevents the adhesive drying out too quickly. Seal the sides as well so that the silver paint will stick better.

2 Measure the diameter of the inside of the saucer and, with a compass, draw a circle of the same size on a piece of brown paper. Cut the circle out with scissors. Draw the design on to the brown paper. You can trace the design from an enlarged copy of the template on page 123 or copy it freehand with charcoal. The precise spacing of the waves will be generated by the spacing and laying of the tiles so the drawing will act as a guide rather than an exact image.

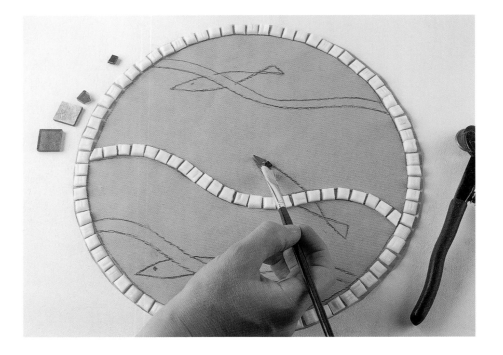

3 Cut the tiles into quarters (see techniques on page 18) and start laying the white border and central wave line. Stick the pieces down with a roughly 50:50 mix of washable PVA and water, applying a small area to the paper with a small paintbrush. To make the fish you will find that double-wheel tile cutters will cut the silver tiles more accurately and with less wastage.

4 Continue laying the waves working up and down from the center wave line, leaving out the tiles around the fish until you are able to lay the upper and lower white wave lines. Once these are in you can lay the other two fish and cut the wave tiles to fit around them.

5 When the tiles are all fixed to the paper and the glue is dry you are ready to fix the mosaic to the saucer. First mix the grout with water into a thick paste and spread it across the back of the mosaic using your hands protected in rubber gloves, working the grout into the joints between the tiles.

6 Sponge the back of the tiles clean with a damp tiler's sponge. Make sure the sponge isn't too wet as this will wash the grout out of the joints and also make the mosaic too wet and fragile. Squeeze the sponge out and always use a clean face of the sponge for every wipe so as not to spread the grout back onto the tiles. Filling the joints with grout in this way, known as pre-grouting, stops the adhesive from coming up between the joints and also helps loosen the bond of the tiles to the paper while giving extra suction to the bond between the tiles and the adhesive.

7 Setting the mosaic to one side, mix up the cement-based adhesive to a thick paste and immediately spread onto the base of the saucer with a small notched trowel to achieve an even thickness of adhesive across the surface.

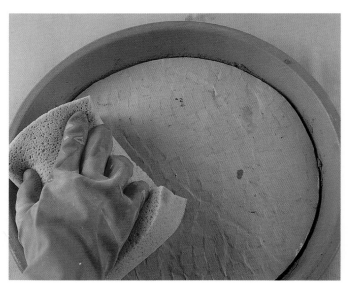

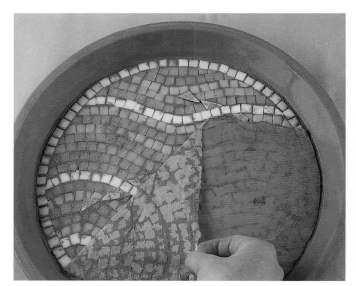

8 Turn the pre-grouted mosaic over into the adhesive bed and press down firmly across the whole area. This can be done with your fingers or with a damp sponge. Keep wetting the back of the paper with the damp (but not wet) sponge until the water has penetrated and the paper turns a darker color.

9 Carefully lift an edge of the paper and, if it peels easily, continue to pull it back, parallel to the surface of the mosaic so as not to pull the tiles upwards and out of contact with the adhesive. If at first the paper is still sticking to the tiles you must be patient and wait a little longer.

10 When the paper has been removed it is important to sponge the face of the tiles clean while the grout is still wet and the excess can be lifted easily. The adhesive will also be wet so the mosaic must be treated gently. Adjustments can also be made at this stage if pieces need re-aligning slightly or recutting.

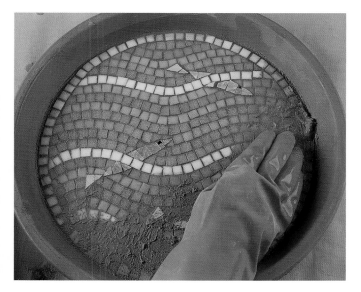

11 When the adhesive is dry, usually in about 12 hours depending on the air temperature and humidity, the piece will need a final grout to fill in any little holes. Cover the whole area with a thick paste as before, and work it in with your fingers protected with rubber gloves. This will fill in any little holes and also the gap around the edge where the mosaic meets the upstand of the saucer. Sponge clean with a damp tiler's sponge, using a clean face for every wipe so as not to spread the grout back over the face of the tiles.

12 When the mosaic is clean and dry, cut out another piece of brown paper slightly larger than the one used to make the mosaic on. This will cover both the mosaic and the grout joint around the perimeter allowing you to spray paint the saucer without covering the mosaic. The paint will dry within one hour after which the bird bath can be filled with water.

Aluminium frame

Waterproof backing board

Powder filler with good adhesion for exterior use

Compass

Ruler

Side-tile nippers

Old pair of nippers

Sheet of brown paper

Washable PVA

3mm notched trowel

Flat bed squeegee

Tiler's sponge

Bucket for water

Pair of rubber gloves

Exterior cement based adhesive (must be suitable for use on wood)

circle panel

The design for this panel stems from a series of works made using circles. The aim was to build unpredictability into a formal and highly predictable structure. The mosaic is made from a mixture of vitreous glass and broken china. A sixth of each circle is picked out in a related but contrasting series of colors, creating a beam-like effect. The angles of orientation of the beams are laid randomly from one circle to the next. Every circle, made mostly from vitreous glass, also includes a certain amount of ceramic tableware. Patterns decorating the surface of the tableware have been cut out and placed, either to complement each other or as a contrast to the accompanying colors. The panel has been made by the indirect method. It might seem curious to work in reverse when it seems so much easier to make the mosaic the right way round and see the immediate effect but the reason lies in the complexity of the design. Sticking small tiles, many of which have a beveled face, to a timber substrate, is a long-winded and tricky process. Working indirect is far faster and mistakes are much easier to correct.

1 This mosaic has been laid on to a board to which the fixings have already been attached – a pair of interlocking battens. For extra security, once the piece is mounted it is possible to screw from the upper into the lower interlocking timber batten. A strip of timber at the base of the panel has been added to ensure an even distance of top and bottom from the wall.

2 Draw a series of circles on the paper with a pair of compasses. Place the compasses on the edge of one circle, at the same distance as that of the radius to the edge, and draw another circle. Do the same again at the point where the first circle intersects with the second, and continue until the whole sheet of paper is covered with intersecting circles. Here, a series were chosen as significant (marked in red) and a pie-slice angle was drawn in from the center of each to the point of intersection on the edge. These slice-like "beams" have also been marked in red – a reminder of where the color changes will occur.

3 Make a selection of vitreous tiles for each circle, with ones of a contrasting series of colors to make up the beams. When choosing, it helps to line up a selection of tiles and check how they inter-relate. Making sure the color relationships work well is critical at this stage, as the mosaic is to be laid in reverse – the patterns will not be seen as the mosaic is being made. Ceramic tableware is easy to cut but blunts nippers quickly, so use an old pair. The ceramic needs to match the size of the glass tiles. Cut a piece of paper fractionally smaller than the board.

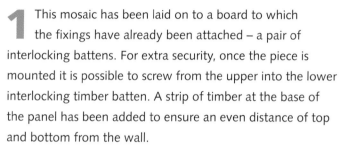

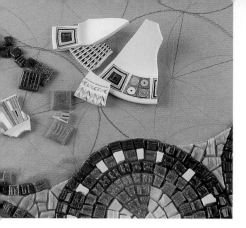

4 Start laying tiles from the outside of each circle inwards. At the point where the colors change, pay careful attention to the cutting or a messy-looking line can result. The blue areas between the circles have been laid with a crazy-laid style of cutting, which allows no circle to have greater linear emphasis than another.

5 Place the mosaic, now stuck to the sheet of paper, within the frame recess. This helps to hold the mosaic in place whilst grouting. Given that the materials used are of varying thicknesses, use your hands protected in rubber gloves to grout the mosaic. Sponge away the excess grout and rinse the sponge regularly. With a slightly curving motion, run the full flat of it across the mosaic. Use each side only once, rinse, squeeze dry and repeat until the mosaic is clean. Be gentle as any tile of a greater height may be torn from the paper. If this should happen, fix with adhesive once the paper has been removed.

6 If there are variations in height, "feather up" to the thicker tiles. This means applying a small quantity of adhesive to the back of the mosaic, to create a smooth, even, if not level, surface. Mix the white cement-based adhesive and apply with a 3 mm notched trowel to the primed, dry surface of the board. Once the adhesive is evenly distributed, turn over the pre-grouted mosaic and carefully place, paper-side-up, into the recess. Take the clean flat-bed squeegee and tap the mosaic into place, ensuring proper contact with the adhesive throughout. Wet with a damp sponge. Re-wet if the surface of the paper begins to dry out.

7 Peel the paper from the face of the tiles and try to keep the paper in a single piece. Clean the mosaic gently with a sponge, then leave to dry. If the beam areas of the circle seem too muted in relation to the colors around them, it is possible to regrout them carefully using a darker tone. This can create an added sense of drama to a design. Remember, it is far easier to regrout with a darker tone than a lighter one, so make the preliminary grout the lightest one likely to be required. When regrouting is complete, buff up the surface and hang outside.

tools and materials

Waterproof plywood board with hardwood frame

Paint for frame and reverse of board

Paintbrush

Ruler

Pencil

Pair of compasses

Tile nippers

Washable PVA

Small brush for glue

Sturdy tile nippers for marble

Light tile nippers for cutting smalti (wheeled nippers are ideal)

Brown paper

Tiler's sponge

3 mm (⅛ in) notched trowel

Flat-bed squeegee

Smalti

Marble

smalti marble wall strip

Smalti and marble have contrasting characteristics. Smalti is a reflective hand-made glass. The changing technology of color production has meant that over the years the material has become purer of hue and less granular in nature. The slightly sandy speckles observable in the vitreous material are seen less frequently in the smalti held by most suppliers, and although manufacturers produce an enormous range of colors, suppliers tend to stock the most intense tones. This purity can make smalti seem rather overwhelming when used on a small scale as a single color. It looks at its best either in combination with closely similar tones of the material itself, or contrasted with marble, whose light-absorbent properties act as an excellent foil to the reflectivity of the hand-made glass. It is important to sound a note of warning: mosaic making is generally not similar to painting – unlike the dabs of color applied by the strokes of a brush, where a range of hues may fuse into a single vibrant surface, the application of grout causes these points to separate – but smalti, generally being ungrouted, acts differently. Smalti can be used outside, but if so, it must either be grouted or bedded deeply enough into adhesive or sand and cement to guard against water penetrating the joints, freezing and causing the material to fail. This panel is intended to work with the soft colors of a brick wall and conveys a sense of the flickering tones of light. Using a series of abstract forms, the design aims to suggest earth, water and sky, whilst the vertical lines springing from the base of the panel, relate to the idea of growth.

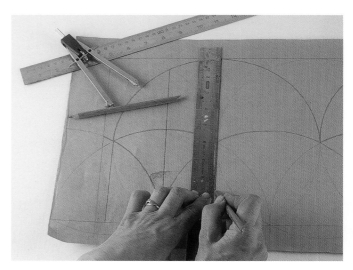

1 The mosaic is laid onto a waterproof plywood board, framed with a hard wood suitable for exterior use. Brass fixings attaching the L-shaped battens have been secured from the front of the board to ensure against water entry and prevent rust. While you paint the frame, apply masking tape to the edge of the board to prevent paint from ruining the surface. Make sure the paint is suitable for exterior use. Varnish or paint the back of the board and the timber L-shaped battens.

2 Cut a piece of brown paper to fit frame. Lay out the circles with a pair of compasses. This design is based on precisely three background semi-circles. The arrangement of circles at the base has a pleasing asymmetry.

3 Make a selection of colors. Here, the brown and mushroom tones of the marble, powerful in themselves, play a recessive and almost neutral role, as their inner, rather than polished face is to be used. The light-absorbent surface contrasts with the fractured, light-reflective face of the glass. A pink smalti has been chosen to echo a note of pink in the mushroom marble (breccia tavira), and blues were selected of a similar tone to that of the brown marble (marron). Smalti can be purchased in plate form (i.e. in large pizza sized plates), but also ready cut into small rectangles. These small rectangles have been cut in half here. The long marble rod is cut into small pieces to match the size of the smalti cubes. Both marble and smalti have a slightly broken, not entirely flat surface. Out of caution, it is probably a good idea to use a slightly stronger mix of glue and water in these circumstances – perhaps 60:40. The absorbent surface of the marble makes it difficult to peel off the paper if the glue is too thick.

4 Start by laying the principal elements of the design – in this case the verticals and the upper setting-out arch of the semi-circles. There is an important point to make here. As a design develops, it is helpful to examine the work with a critical eye. Here, where the vertical lines meet the white background they were initially darker than the verticals laid against the blues and browns (as shown) on the basis that backlit colors darken up against a light source. This was a rational approach, but once the white was laid, it looked less effective than a lighter selection of colors (as shown in Step 5), so a change was made. Understanding that changes are part of the mosaic-making process is invaluable and is a point that guides to the process often overlooked, for understandable reasons. The linear, or "string" border, is light below, and dark above – a reversal of the color treatment of the design within.

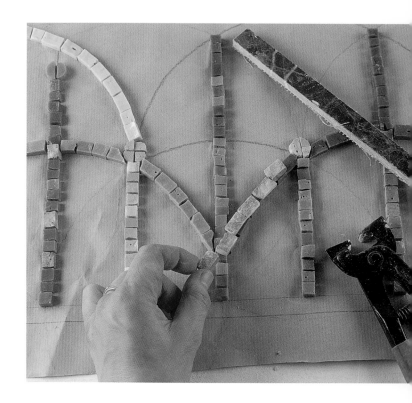

5 For any design using fans or curves of this kind, start at the outside line and work inwards. It can be helpful to draw guidelines to follow, as the rows of tessarae diminish in size towards the center of the circle. These lines are an invaluable aid to beginner and professional alike, for at the point where a line interrupts a circle, it is easy to lose the elegant continuity of the curve. A guideline ensures continued awareness of any variation of shape.

6 Retaining continuity of flow is trickiest where the line is interrupted. To make the task as easy as possible, cut the angles at both ends of the line before filling in with straight-cut tiles. This makes the rest of the cutting simple straight cuts, and protects against ending up with a series of clumsy triangular cuts at the end of a line.

7 Most of this design depends on curves. Where a contrasting element is introduced, it can be helpful to create a subtle replay of the idea elsewhere so the contrast is integrated into the whole. Here, the note of contrast to the curves is the series of vertical lines. Instead of making all the background, or "field", in curves, some straight lines are laid on a horizontal axis, to provide a visual connection between the two elements.

8 When the mosaic is complete, leave it to dry. Once dry, cautiously turn the mosaic over, checking to ensure the material is safely stuck, with the aim of displacing any shards that may have become trapped between the tiles. Do this on a clean surface, so that any tile that falls out is not lost, and can be re-stuck. Although this may seem risky, it is much better to do it at this point than to risk it occurring during the process of fixing, when it can lead to real problems. Butter the back of the smalti with a thick layer of adhesive. Used outside, smalti needs to be bonded really well to prevent water damage. As this mosaic is not to be grouted, the adhesive will protect the surface against the elements, so it is critically important that every tile is soundly bedded. Working on paper, minor variations in thickness of the material have the potential to hold the thinner tiles high, preventing contact with the adhesive. To guard against this, it is essential a thick layer of adhesive is applied over the smalti to create an even surface.

9 Apply adhesive to the board using the notched trowel. The manufacturers of this particular adhesive recommend the board is left unprimed. It is essential to follow manufacturers' recommendations, which may vary depending on the content of the adhesive. Pick up the mosaic, now coated with a thick layer of adhesive, but minimize the amount you touch the buttered surface.

10 Once the mosaic has been turned over and positioned on the board, wet the paper with a damp sponge. Leave to absorb moisture until the paper can be peeled away with ease. This might take anything from five minutes to half an hour, depending on a number of factors – strength of glue, humidity, etc. If the paper starts to dry out, re-wet. When the paper is ready, remove it. It can be helpful to start in one corner, and try to remove it in a single piece. The absorbent surface of riven marble (marble with a broken, unpolished face) can make removing the paper trickier than it would be if the entire mosaic was made in smalti. Be prepared to be patient and for the process to take time. The mosaic should not be left to cure with the paper on the front. If there are problems – for example at the spots where the mosaic was held in order to be reversed – then these need dealing with while the adhesive still permits.

11 When the paper has been removed, tap the mosaic thoroughly with a flat trowel, ensuring a good bond between the two layers of adhesive. This tapping can even up the surface, so that if one area seems low (as it may be at the spots where the mosaic was held) adhesive can be gently pushed across to even out the difference between low and high spots. Part of the appeal of smalti is the fractured, uneven face – it is not advisable to aim for an absolutely flat finish. Clean the surface thoroughly with a wet sponge and a fresh bucket of water. There will be deposits of glue on the face of the tiles, which must be removed. Remove the masking tape. Leave to dry, before placing in the garden.

tools and materials

Brown paper

Black and white ceramic tiles

Tile nippers

Washable PVA glue

Small paintbrush

52 cm (20 in) diameter circle of tile-backer board

Gray grout

Gray cement-based adhesive

Tiler's sponge

Grouter's float

Notched trowel

night and day roundel

This black and white design makes an attractive centerpiece in a patio or a decorative stepping stone in a lawn or flowerbed. It is made of unglazed ceramic tiles fixed to tile-backer board to create a durable and hard-wearing surface that can be walked on so long as the board is fully supported underneath on a sand or cement bed. The design is inspired by the medieval floor mosaics which are found in churches throughout Europe and in particular profusion in northern Italy. Made of a limited palette of marble colors, often only black and white, these floor designs often display a particularly vigorous graphic style and are full of character and movement. In the Middle Ages floor mosaics were considered less important than wall decorations which were usually executed by itinerant Byzantine mosaicists. It was therefore left to local craftsmen to make these marble pavements and this is reflected in the variety and quirkiness of the mosaic styles. The subject matter was also less elevated, avoiding Biblical or religious themes in favor of illustrations of more everyday phenomena, such as the months and the seasons, as well as the more exotic elements of the medieval imagination, such as dragons, griffins and chimera. They communicate a uniquely vivid picture of the preoccupations of ordinary medieval life, but they seem to have fallen from fashion in the 12th century and almost all were covered over with later, plainer, and less obviously secular and superstitious floor coverings. The world they reflect is now a very foreign and distant place but we are still profoundly influenced by some of the same natural rhythms, most obviously the regular cycle from day to night, which is the subject of this panel.

1 Cut a circle of brown paper to the size of the tile-backer board and draw on the design. You can trace the design from an enlarged copy of the template on page 125 or copy it freehand with charcoal or pencil. Remember that in the indirect method the image you draw will be the reverse of the finished mosaic.

2 Cut some quarters of black and white ceramic (see techniques on page 18) and start sticking down to the paper using a roughly 50:50 mix of washable PVA with water. Apply the glue with a small paintbrush to a small area of paper, starting with the outside border. Leave a gap in the border at the bottom so that you can sweep out the cut fragments as you work. Move on to the tree, the animals, and the sun and moon, trying to avoid using very small pieces. You can often use two three-quarter sized pieces instead of one whole and a small piece, and this will look neater as well as avoiding the difficulty of fixing very small pieces which can be difficult to stick down successfully.

3 To fill in the background using the haphazard technique used in this project it is useful to have a variety of different sized squares and rectangles to fill in the variety of shapes with a minimum of special cutting and shaping. Therefore when you are cutting down from the bigger tiles do not aim for equal quarters but for a variety of shapes.

4 The lines of laying roughly follow the outlines of the motifs and the areas in between are filled with a variety of rectangles and squares, tilted and arranged to fill the spaces. The grout gaps are sometimes quite large but the consistent approach creates a kind of unforced order that would be hard to achieve following a more tightly organized system.

5 When the tiles are all fixed to the paper and the glue is dry you are ready to fix the mosaic to the tile-backer board. First, mix the grout with water into a thick paste and spread it across the back of the mosaic using your hands protected in rubber gloves, working the grout into the joints between the tiles.

6 Then sponge the back of the tiles clean with a damp tiler's sponge. Make sure the sponge isn't too wet, as this will wash the grout out of the joints and also make the mosaic too wet and fragile. Squeeze the sponge out and always use a clean face of the sponge for every wipe so as not to spread the grout back onto the tiles. Filling the joints with grout in this way, known as pre-grouting, stops the adhesive from coming up between the joints and also helps loosen the bond of the tiles to the paper while giving extra suction to the bond between the tiles and the adhesive.

7 Set the mosaic to one side and mix up the cement-based adhesive to a thick paste and immediately spread onto the tile-backer board with a notched trowel to achieve an even thickness of adhesive across the surface.

8 Turn the pre-grouted mosaic over into the adhesive bed and press down firmly across the whole area. This can be done with a grouter's float which provides even pressure over a flat surface. Keep wetting the back of the paper with a damp (but not wet) sponge until the water has penetrated and the paper turns a darker color.

9 While waiting for the water to sink in and the glue to dissolve you can run some adhesive around the edge of the mosaic. The adhesive will be kept off the face of the mosaic by the brown paper and it will strengthen the vulnerable edge of both the mosaic and the backer board.

night and day roundel

10 Carefully lift an edge of the paper and if, it peels easily, continue to pull it back, parallel to the surface of the mosaic so as not to pull the tiles upwards and out of contact with the adhesive. The paper may tear into sections as you work but this is not a problem. It may be easier to take the paper off in smaller sections than in a single sheet. When the paper has been removed it is important to sponge the face of the tiles clean while the grout is still wet and the excess can be lifted easily. The adhesive will also be wet so the mosaic must be treated gently. Adjustments can also be made at this stage if pieces need re-aligning slightly or recutting.

11 When the adhesive is dry, usually in about twelve hours depending on the air temperature and humidity, the piece will need a final grout to fill in any little holes. Cover the whole area with a thick paste as before, and work it in with your fingers protected with rubber gloves.

12 Sponge clean with a damp tiler's sponge, using a clean face for every wipe so as not to spread the grout back over the face of the tiles.

tools and materials

- Stainless steel or brass ring
- Builder's washed sand
- Cement
- Sturdy tile nippers
- Brown paper
- Washable PVA glue
- Tiler's sponge
- 2 buckets: 1 for mixing, 1 for water
- Mixing trowel
- Flat-bed squeegee
- Gray colored grout
- Pencil
- Small glue brush
- Marble rods
- Limestone
- Smalti
- Rubber gloves
- Cement-based adhesive

cast slab

The design for this mosaic is based on a material that is conventionally supplied to be hand-cut into mosaic cubes – marble rods. Although mosaic designs are often made with cubes of a similar size or scale, or with a similar surface (matte or shiny) pleasing results can result from contrasting some of these elements. Instead of aligning the rods, they have been cut and laid at angles to one another, producing an effect rather reminiscent of Constructivism – the early 20th century art movement based on geometric abstraction, often identified with dramatic angular juxtapositions, contrasts of dark and light, and conveying awareness of an industrial world. The palette here is softer, but the design has a frenzied, angular quality quite unlike the gentler, more painterly style of mosaic that looks back to Byzantine precedents. On completion, this mosaic roundel is beaten into sand and cement, a very practical substrate for exterior use. Set into this stainless steel ring, the mosaic could either be used as a table top placed on cast iron legs (although the table top would be undeniably heavy) or laid as a decorative feature as part of a paving scheme.

1 It is not essential to have an edging strip manufactured for a paving mosaic but it does make for a neat edge. Brass and stainless steel rings are equally effective. If an edging strip cannot be sourced, cut some light flexible sheet material (like shuttering ply) to create a circular structure onto which to cast the base. The height of the ply should be that of the base, plus the thickest material used in the mosaic, plus one millimeter. Ensure that the top edge is absolutely level. The finished mosaic will be leveled to this edge, so any inconsistencies here will show. The shuttering ply must be nailed onto a base – any scrap timber will do. Curve and tap the ply into position, following the line of a circle drawn to the requisite size on the base board. A beam compass is a useful tool for this purpose. Mark a piece of brown paper to the inner dimensions of the plywood ring. Make a registration mark, both on the paper and on the ring of metal or ply.

2 If you are working with a shuttering mold, rub the sides and base with petroleum jelly to prevent the slab bonding with the timber. If using a metal ring, rub only the base as it is desirable that the concrete adheres to the surrounding ring. Drill four holes in the ring at even intervals and place a screw through each. These will be held in position by the concrete base, preventing the ring from slipping free from the mosaic it encloses. For the concrete mix, use three parts sand, two parts aggregate (pea shingle has been used here) and one part cement. Mix the dry ingredients thoroughly to ensure the concrete is not too weak, then make a well in the center and add water. Do not add too much water – the mix should be able to support itself when heaped up on the trowel. Fill the circle to a point 1 mm below the depth of the thickest material used. Create a gauge to ensure the surface is perfectly even: take a piece of timber fractionally longer than the diameter of the circle. Cut two slots out of the timber to the thickness of the required height. Move the gauge in a circular motion to ensure an absolutely flat surface. Set aside to dry for one week.

3 Make a selection of materials. Here, the mosaic is keyed to the soft colors of the marble, but working with a delicate palette of green and gray marble and yellow limestone, some rather more vivid colors of smalti (a light turquoise and greeny yellow) have been chosen to add a more brilliant note. A number of the materials have a polished finish, whilst others are matte. The contrast adds to the dynamism of the design.

4 Cut the rods roughly to size, and then fine-tune the cuts. It can be helpful, as with other mosaic materials, to draw the cutting line onto the marble with a pencil.

5 The design is based on a number of rules. A series of V shapes are laid out, at regular intervals, but not necessarily in alignment with one another, in order to give a sense of movement. The Vs are laid in pale green and botticino marble, and a line of matte French limestone shadows one side of each.

6 Continue cutting, drawing and laying the material. Here, smalti has been laid with the pitted, inner face exposed. This is not generally recommended for flooring, as the fractured face can become dirty, and the material is thinner than the marble, whereas laid on its side, its thickness exactly matches that of marble. This panel is to be laid on an urban roof terrace, and the client will be made conscious of how to maintain it, so the decision to use the inner face was made for aesthetic reasons. Even so, the panel must be protected with stone sealant and cleaned regularly. Over time, used outside, the polished face of marble gradually dulls. It is possible to delay this process by careful maintenance, but it is an aging process one has to accept.

7 When finished, set aside to dry and prepare for the fixing process. When the mosaic is dry, start to fix. This process will take at least one hour, so ensure you have enough time before beginning. Mix the grout with water into a thick paste and spread it across the back of the mosaic using your hands protected in rubber gloves, working the grout into the joints between the tiles. When the entire mosaic has been grouted, sponge off the excess. Wet the sponge and squeeze it out until it is as dry as possible. With a slightly curving motion, run the full flat of the sponge across the mosaic to maximize the surface area. Use each side of the sponge only once. When all the sides of the sponge have been used, wash it out in a bucket of clean water and repeat the operation until the mosaic is clean.

8 When the mosaic has been sponged clean and the joints grouted, mix up the adhesive. It is also possible to make a cement slurry to adhere the mosaic to the base, but in this case, a cement-based adhesive has been used. Butter the back of the mosaic with a thick layer of adhesive. The aim is to create a level surface.

9 Next, apply adhesive (or slurry) to the dry surface of the concrete base. Once the adhesive is evenly distributed, pick up the pre-grouted mosaic, turn it over, and carefully place, paper-side up, into the ring. Take the clean flat-bed squeegee and tap the mosaic into place, ensuring proper contact with the adhesive throughout.

cast slab

10 Wet the sponge and do not squeeze it out to the same extent as before. Wet the paper thoroughly and leave to absorb the moisture. This may take about ten minutes. If the paper starts to dry during this period, re-wet with the sponge. When the paper has changed from a light to a dark color and has clearly absorbed the moisture, peel it off, starting from one side. The ring helps hold the mosaic into position, so the paper can be removed in a single piece from one side only. Once all the paper has been removed (this is a slightly trickier task when using unpolished marble, as it retains the glue more than other materials) tap the whole of the mosaic with the flat-bed squeegee, vigorously, until an absolutely flat surface is achieved. The mosaic must be both flat, and flush with the edge.

11 Regrout once the mosaic is level and sound. Avoid leaving any small holes in the grout, as water may pool at these spots.

12 Clean off. Leave to dry. Once dry, the mosaic within a ring can be laid in the garden. The unframed mosaic can be removed from its shuttering, and the edges retouched with grout. Once dry, it can be placed in its desired position.

- Brown paper
- Charcoal
- Washable PVA glue
- Small paintbrush
- Unglazed ceramic tiles
- Vitreous glass tiles
- Tile nippers
- Double-wheel tile cutters
- Ceramic floor tile
- Gray grout
- Gray cement-based adhesive
- Notched trowel
- Tiler's sponge
- Mixing trowel
- Rubber gloves

flying jay wall plaque

This design is inspired directly by nature and the increasingly common sight in urban towns and gardens of an unexpected flash of color as a jay swoops along from tree to tree. The process of transforming a real object or creature into a successful mosaic can be approached in two distinct ways. There is the highly realistic approach, championed by the Vatican schools in Rome, who have, since the time of Raphael, used mosaic with enormous skill to emulate the effects achieved in painting. This technique uses very careful shading and foreshortening effects to create the illusion of a three dimensional object on what is really a flat surface. This approach is often tempting when trying to capture the appearance of a real creature and when using photographs or natural history illustrations as reference materials. However, the particular characteristics of mosaic make these illusions difficult to achieve, unless working with very small pieces, and then the amount of labor involved can raise the question of why not do a painting or take a photograph instead. The other approach is to stylise the natural forms, capturing their spirit but not their exact detail. In this project, the feathers of the jay have been simplified to create a regular pattern formed from the repeating shapes and colors of the mosaic pieces. The scale of this pattern is much larger than the pattern of the real jay's feathers, but the aim is to communicate the beauty of the pattern-making and the sense of underlying order. The background is a simple motif of twigs and catkins that breaks up the pale blue of the sky. This area is treated with great simplicity, in a single color and with regular shaped pieces, so as not to conflict with the complexity of the bird which is the focus of the piece.

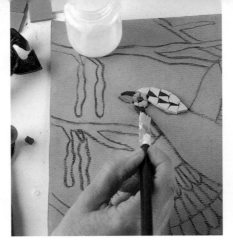

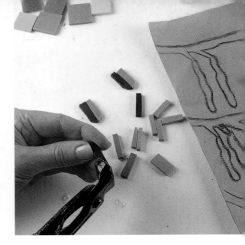

1 Draw the design in reverse on a piece of brown paper cut to the size of the floor tile. You can trace the design from an enlarged copy of the template on page 124 or copy it freehand with charcoal or pencil. Remember that in the indirect method the image you draw will be the reverse of the finished mosaic. Also bear in mind as you draw the size of the mosaic tiles so that where possible the different elements of the pattern can be cut easily from halves and quarters. At this stage you should also select your colors. The bird and twigs are made from unglazed ceramics, while the sky is made from vitreous glass. Small pieces of vitreous glass are also used for the blue in the feathers and around the eye.

2 Start with the head of the bird. When making a creature of any kind it is always a good idea to start with the head as this will give it character and life from the start. Apply a small amount of washable PVA (diluted 50:50 with water) to the brown paper with a small paintbrush.

3 The body of the bird and some of the wings are made of long, narrow strips of unglazed ceramic. These are most easily cut with double-wheel tile cutters. Further shaping and the nibbling required to make the curved ends of the feathers is best done with tile nippers.

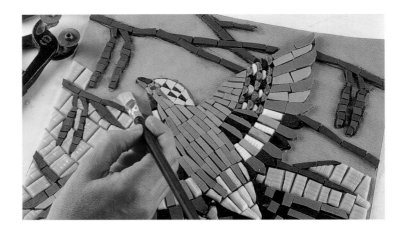

4 The twigs are also made with narrow strips cut with the double-wheel tile cutters. The strips are more effective if they taper slightly as this creates a line of uneven thickness that suggests the organic growth of the twig. The lines of laying for the sky follow the lines of the twigs, reinforcing the dynamic angled flight of the bird. It is made up of slightly skew-cut halves, which makes it possible to follow the slight wobbles of the twigs.

5 When the tiles are fixed to the paper and the glue is dry, fix the mosaic to the ceramic floor tile. First, mix the grout with water into a thick paste and spread it across the back of the mosaic, using your hands protected in rubber gloves, working the grout into the joints between the tiles. Sponge the back of the tiles clean with a damp tiler's sponge. Always use a clean face of the sponge for every wipe so as not to spread the grout back on to the tiles. Set the mosaic to one side.

6 Mix the cement-based adhesive to a thick paste and spread onto the ceramic tile with a notched trowel to achieve a regular thin bed of adhesive across the surface. This can be tricky as the adhesive does not want to stick to the smooth surface of the tile. If the mosaic is not too large it is possible to place the substrate on top of the mosaic. First slip a small board under the mosaic, then carefully turn the tile over and place on top of the pre-grouted mosaic. Hold the board and tile tightly together and turn them over so that the tile is now lying on the work surface and the paper facing upwards.

7 You can now damp the paper and press the mosaic down onto the tile. A mixing trowel is used here as a tool with which to apply the necessary firm and even pressure. Keep wetting the back of the paper with a damp (but not wet) sponge until the water has penetrated and the paper turns a darker color. While waiting for the water to sink in and the glue to dissolve, run some adhesive around the vulnerable edge of the mosaic to strengthen it.

8 Lift an edge of the paper and pull it back, parallel to the surface of the mosaic so as not to pull the tiles upwards and out of contact with the adhesive. When the paper has been removed, gently sponge the face of the tiles clean while the grout is still wet and the excess can be lifted easily. Re-align or recut any pieces now, if necessary. When the adhesive is dry, cover the area with a thick paste of grout, and work it in with your fingers protected with rubber gloves and then sponge clean with a damp tiler's sponge as

TO MAKE THE SLABS:

Casting frame

Masking tape

Petroleum jelly

Builder's washed sand

Cement

**2 buckets: 1 for mixing,
1 for water**

Notched trowel

Tiler's sponge

Small tiles used as spacers

Rubber gloves

FOR SEAT ONCE SLABS
HAVE BEEN PREPARED:

Blue tiles

Vitreous tiles

Cement-based adhesive

Small plasterer's trowel

Bucket for water

Rubber gloves

Anthracite colored grout

Tiler's sponge

seat

The mosaic applied to this seat is laid by the direct method. The seat itself is constructed from cast concrete slabs, intersected with lines of brilliant glass mosaic. The idea owes something to the 20th century architectural modernist idea of "truth to materials" – in which the properties inherent to any substance are exposed, rather than disguised, and materials are not made to mimic one another. Any pitting or blemish produced in the process of casting the concrete has been left visible. The differing characteristics of the two materials are mutually complementary. Concrete can be a dusty surface on which to sit, so a slab of granite of a similar size has been used as the seat itself. A polished concrete top would probably be the most attractive finish, but not everyone may find it easy to source a concrete polishing machine. Granite pavers on the other hand, are readily available from tile shops and garden centers.

1 Cast a series of slabs (see techniques on page 23) or buy a number of appropriately sized concrete pavers from a garden center. Source some small tiles to use as spacers between the cast slabs (high fired floor tiles are inexpensive and suitable, although small marble tiles have been used here). It is important that the height of the spacers is fractionally greater than that of a single 2 cm vitreous tile, and so these 1 cm tiles have been paired. It is of course possible to custom-make the spacers, casting them to the required size.

2 Ensure the edges of the pavers are thoroughly protected with masking tape. Creating a fixing bed for the mosaic is a messy business, and the surface of the cast concrete would be considerably less attractive if coated with adhesive.

3 Tape the granite slab to be used for the top of the seat. Unlike marble, the surface of granite does not become muted over time. It will retain its polished finish.

4 Mix cement-based adhesive to a stiff paste and place the spacers in each corner. Ensure each spacer is coated with adhesive above and below. Fill between the spacers to give support, but it is not necessary to fill the entire area with adhesive. The seat will be heavy – do not make it heavier than necessary.

5 When the seat has been assembled, create the adhesive bed onto which the mosaic is to be fixed.

6 Use a tile as a gauge, ensuring there is a perfect space for tile and fixing bed, removing any surplus, or supplementing with adhesive if the fixing bed is a little low.

7 These vitreous tiles have been cut at an angle, giving a pleasing sense of irregularity to an otherwise ordered structure. Some of the tiles are blue, others are vitreous glass. Both the front and the reverse glass faces have been used. The tiles are placed into a bed of adhesive, applied a small amount at a time with a putty knife or small trowel (see Step 5). Take care to stick the tiles firmly, but do not press so hard that adhesive squeezes up between the joints. A different selection of materials has been used for each side of the seat. When completed, leave the adhesive time to cure, before attempting to grout.

8 When the adhesive has cured, mix a tub of grout to a stiff paste and grout with a gloved hand. This is easier than a large unwieldy grouting squeegee. Sponge clean, buff up the surface, remove the masking tape and leave to dry before placing in position.

tools and materials

- Brown paper
- Compass
- Charcoal
- Vitreous glass tiles
- Unglazed ceramic tiles
- Double-wheel tile cutters
- Tile nippers
- Pencil
- Rubber gloves
- Gray grout
- Tiler's sponge
- Exterior grade circular plywood board (40 cm/ 16 in diameter)
- Gray cement-based adhesive
- Notched trowel
- Grouter's float or mixing trowel
- Heavy-duty double-sided tape
- Scalpel or hobby knife
- Copper edge strip
- Copper hardboard pins

runner bean

This design was inspired by a page in an Italian herbal dating from the 14th century. The illustrator was called Serapion the Younger and he was amongst the first artists to break with the medieval tradition of copying from earlier manuscripts in favor of drawing directly from nature. The result, however, is not a portrait of a plant as you would see it growing in the garden, but a careful composition that shows all the elements of the plant – roots, leaves, flowers and fruit, – separated out and combined in a single image. This reflects the new scientific interests of the time and the fascination with the underlying structures of nature as well as with detailed observation. The history of botanical illustration is full of inspiring images and one of their great values for the mosaic designer is the clarity of the forms laid out against the blank page. The exquisite detail of these drawings may be impossible to capture in mosaic but the strength of the compositions and the interest of the shapes makes them excellent mosaic subjects. This circular panel has a simple design but it needs to be made with careful cutting to achieve an elegant effect. It uses vitreous glass for the plant itself and white unglazed ceramic for the background. The single color of the background echoes the plain paper of the original illustration but it is given interest by laying the pieces to a pattern of concentric circles whose regularity creates a dynamic contrast with the organic asymmetry of the bean. The finished piece could be used either as a little table on metal or hardwood legs, or as a panel hung on the wall.

1 Cut a piece of brown paper to the same size as the exterior plywood backing board. Draw on the design using charcoal or trace it from an enlarged version of the template on page 125. You will also find it helpful to draw some concentric circles with a compass to help with the laying of the background – circles can go surprisingly awry without guidelines to follow. To find the center of the circle fold the piece of paper in half and then half again. It is unnecessary to work out exactly where the rows will lie in advance as randomly spaced circles will provide enough of a guide when you are laying.

2 The plant shapes are made up of carefully cut pieces. The stems are formed from thin strips cut with double-wheel tile cutters interspersed with small squares of a different shade. The leaves are laid with angled halves positioned to suggest the veins in the leaf's surface, and the flowers are made up of different reds, progressing from rich and dark to intensely bright. The beans are made of alternating shades of green that are close enough to the leaf and stem colors not to break up the overall composition, but different enough to create a subtle separation.

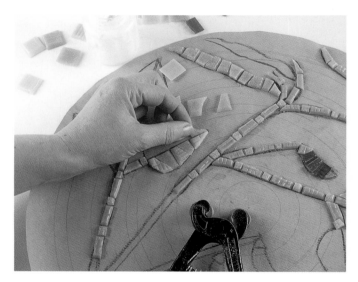

3 To shape these pieces the straight cuts are easiest to make with double-wheel cutters and the curves by nibbling with tile nippers.

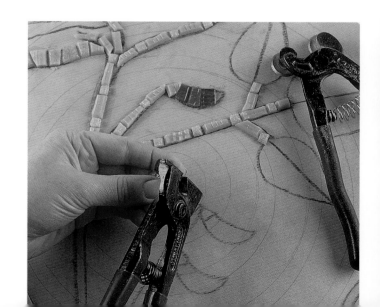

4 The background is laid in concentric circles of alternating rows of long and short strips of white unglazed ceramic which can be cut with either cutting tool. Some slightly angled cuts will be useful in creating the circular rows, and a bit of variety in the widths will add liveliness to the finished effect. Start sticking from the outside edge and work inwards, following the curves of the guidelines. When the rows are interrupted by the plant form, it is a good idea to place the piece on top of the mosaic and mark the line of the necessary cut on the white tile with a pencil. There is a lot of contrast between the white tiles and the grout so the cuts will show up clearly and therefore need to be executed with care. The centerpiece is a circle cut from a single tile, and the preceding row can be adjusted in width to fill the remaining gap.

5 When the tiles are all fixed to the paper and the glue is dry you are ready to fix the mosaic to the exterior plywood base board. First mix the grout with water into a thick paste and spread it across the back of the mosaic using your hands protected in rubber gloves, working the grout into the joints between the tiles.

6 Then sponge the back of the tiles clean with a damp tiler's sponge. Make sure the sponge isn't too wet as this will wash the grout out of the joints and also make the mosaic too wet and fragile. Squeeze the sponge out and always use a clean face of the sponge for every wipe so as not to spread the grout back on to the tiles. Filling the joints with grout in this way, known as pre-grouting, stops the adhesive from coming up between the joints and also helps loosen the bond of the tiles to the paper while giving extra suction to the bond between the tiles and the adhesive.

7 Set the mosaic to one side and mix up the cement-based adhesive to a thick paste and immediately spread onto the plywood board with a notched trowel to achieve an even thickness of adhesive across the surface. Pay particular attention to the edges of the board, ensuring that the adhesive bed is thick enough to hold the vulnerable edge pieces.

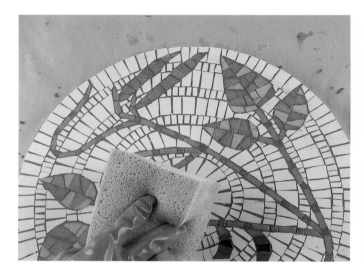

8 Turn the pre-grouted mosaic over into the adhesive bed and press down firmly across the whole area. You can do this with your hands or using a tool such as a grouter's float or a mixing trowel, or with a flat piece of board. Keep wetting the back of the paper with a damp (but not wet) sponge until the water has penetrated and the paper turns a darker color. Carefully lift an edge of the paper and, if it peels easily, continue to pull it back, parallel to the surface of the mosaic so as not to pull the tiles upwards and out of contact with the adhesive. The paper may tear into sections as you work but this is not a problem. It may be easier to take the paper off in smaller sections than in a single sheet.

9 When the paper has been removed it is important to sponge the face of the tiles clean while the grout is still wet and the excess can be lifted easily. The adhesive will also be wet so the mosaic must be treated gently. Adjustments can also be made at this stage if pieces need re-aligning slightly or recutting. Seeing the piece the right way up may reveal awkward cuts or clumsy junctions that can easily be rectified by replacing individual tiles. When the adhesive is dry, usually in about twelve hours depending on the air temperature and humidity, the piece will need a final grout to fill in any little holes. Cover the whole area with a thick paste as before, and work it in with your fingers protected with rubber gloves. Sponge clean with a damp tiler's sponge, using a clean face for every wipe so as not to spread the grout back over the face of the tiles.

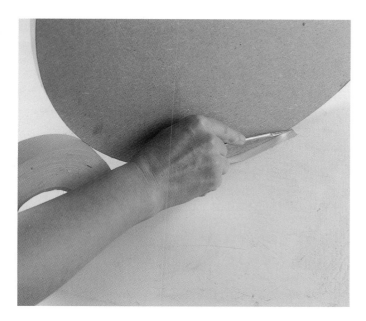

10 When the grout is dry the piece can be framed with copper strip. This is most easily applied if the edge of the board is first covered with a strong double-sided adhesive tape. If the tape is wider than the board it is best to stick it first and then carefully trim off the excess with a scalpel or sharp hobby knife.

11 After removing the protective layer of the sticky tape you can then carefully wind round the copper strip, pressing it into the edge of the board as you go.

12 The tape ensures a tight fit between the copper and the board but it may not provide a permanent bond. The final step is therefore to hammer some small copper hardboard pins into the edge of the board every 15 cm (6 in). Be careful to drive the nails into the center of the board rather than the center of the strip as this may be rather close the mosaic bed and could dislodge the edge tiles.

tools and materials

Sheet of brown paper

Pair of goggles

Small hammer

Backing board

L-shaped wooden edging strip

Saw

Screws

Filler for covering screw holes

Washable PVA

Panel on which to cut slate with hammer

3 mm (⅛ in) notched trowel

Masking tape

Rubber gloves

Tile nippers

Marble

Smalti

Sturdy tile nippers for marble

Wheeled tile nippers for smalti

Small plasterer's tool for applying adhesive to back of tiles

Rubber gloves

wall panel

The starting point for this design was roofing slate – matte in surface and dark in tone. It has been combined with other natural materials, but if used solely with a palette of light colors, the slate would rely for its effect on contrast, and could be in danger of looking heavy and obvious. By combining light and dark tones of slate, marble and terracotta, a visual connection between the materials has been made. An overlapping and layered patchwork of materials and tones helps create a complex sense of space. Both brilliant and softer tones of smalti are combined with the natural materials to introduce an element of reflectivity to the design.

1 Always use protective goggles when cutting. Slate tends to break in unpredictable ways, but if placed on a hard surface the fracture is easier to control. To create a number of small pieces keep the larger part of the slate on the slab and hit hard with a small hammer where it emerges over the slab. If you want to form curves or more intricate shapes in the larger slab, take the hammer and lightly tap at the junction with the edge. External curves are easier to create than internal ones. Stick the small pieces of slate to the paper with washable glue. To disrupt the visual predictability of serried ranks of slate, some have been laid along a different axis.

2 This design was created in a spontaneous way, responding to the materials rather than working through a pre-planned exercise. It is easy to see, by looking at the regular, predictable way in which the slate lies on the paper how the design could have become nothing more than a patchwork of color, with nothing particularly compelling about it. Already though, some tones have been chosen to pick up the color of the slate and to help create a more ambiguous sense of space. Use wheeled cutters to cut the smalti accurately.

3 If the mosaic is to be fixed to a timber base it might seem sensible to start every project by painting the frame and varnishing the back of the board. But it is impossible to paint the frame before one is certain of the balance of colors, as it is important to respond to the materials when selecting the hue of the frame. As white unites the background, white has been selected as the frame color here. Protect the frame with masking tape once it has been painted.

4 This slate is much thinner than the materials surrounding it. With the reverse method, materials of a variety of thickness can be made broadly similar in level. Sometime, in flattening out the material, one can lose a certain amount of character, so some mosaicists prefer to work by the direct method when working with a variety of materials. Thinner materials can be built up with adhesive from the back, and the smalti can retain its uneven character. Here the slate has been given a single, double or triple band of color on one side only, to pick up some characteristics of the adjoining materials. The slate and accompanying band lie in a small field of a brighter or more muted hue.

5 When the design is complete, butter the back of the mosaic with a thick layer of adhesive. As this mosaic is not to be grouted, the adhesive will protect the surface against the elements, so it is critically important that every tile is soundly bedded. Having worked onto paper, minor variations in thickness of the material have the potential to hold the pieces of slate at a distance from the adhesive. To prevent this from happening, it is essential that a thick layer of adhesive is applied to create an even surface.

6 Apply adhesive with the notched trowel to the board. The manufacturers of the adhesive used here recommend the board is left unprimed. It is essential to follow manufacturers' recommendations. Pick up the mosaic, now hidden from view by a thick layer of adhesive. Turn it over, laying it into the notched surface now covering the board. Where mosaic is held, the adhesive will become slightly thinner, so minimize the amount you touch the buttered surface. Once the mosaic has been turned over and positioned on the board, wet the paper with a damp sponge. Leave to absorb moisture until the paper can be peeled away with ease. If the paper starts to dry out, re-wet.

7 When the paper has changed color to a rich dark brown, peel it off. Once removed, cautiously tap the surface of the mosaic to ensure a good bond between the two layers of adhesive. By tapping gently, adhesive can be pushed across to even out the difference between low and high spots. Part of the appeal of smalti is its fractured, uneven face – it is not advisable to aim for an absolutely flat finish. Clean the surface thoroughly with a clean, wet sponge. There will be deposits of glue on the face of the tiles, which must be sponged off. Remove the masking tape applied in Step 3 around the frame. Leave to dry before placing outside.

two beasts under a tree

This decorative wall panel shows a horse and an ox standing under a fruit tree in front of a distant mountain range. The treatment is very stylized, allowing the interest of the mosaic materials and the patterns of laying to be as important to the piece as the mysterious scene itself. The rich and intense colors used were inspired by the vivid colors of medieval manuscripts, whose pigments, hidden from the light inside their protective bindings, retain an astonishing brilliance and vitality. Some glass mosaic colors have a comparable intensity but the process of fixing and grouting often diminishes this brilliance and the change between the ungrouted mosaic and the finished piece can sometimes be heartbreakingly disappointing. When this panel was first fixed the effect seemed too dark and gloomy but as the surface was cleaned and the grout gradually dried it acquired a new kind of intensity. This was due to the transparent glass elements used throughout the piece, which, when bedded in white adhesive, gained a depth and sparkle that restored the overall brilliance of the finished piece. The even arrangement of these pieces in the checkerboard pattern of the laying gives the overall surface an interesting tension between its actual flatness and the visual depth of the transparent glass.

two beasts under a tree

1 If you are designing your own mosaic some forward planning is a good idea. A color sketch will help you to visualize the piece and select your color range. It can be quite small and simple, concentrating on the overall composition and color balance. It is not necessary to plan it in piece by piece detail as this will develop more naturally as you experiment during the process of making.

2 You can scale up and reverse your drawing by making a tracing of the outlines of the design. Turning over the tracing will reverse the image and you can then draw on a grid of squares, in this case dividing the image into 16 blocks.

3 A piece of brown paper cut to the size of the finished piece can then be gridded up into the same number of squares. The image can then be transferred, square by square, to the larger scale. Charcoal is a good tool to use as it can easily be altered so that the image fits together harmoniously and lines run between the squares in a smooth and flowing way.

4 Start laying with the tree. The circular shapes of the fruits and the leaf shapes will be best cut with tile nippers (see techniques on page 18) while the dark brown quarters from which the background is made can be cut with double-wheel tile cutters. The laying of these pieces can be fairly haphazard and the gaps quite big as the dark grout will conceal the joints.

5 The sky is laid in a checker pattern of four different combinations of blue and in each combination one of the colors is translucent and the other opaque. Start laying in rows from the top and work downwards, moving from the dark colors to the lightest. The tiles have been cut into unequal squares and rectangles to allow them to be laid in slightly undulating lines which helps to avoid an over-regular and mechanical effect.

6 The hills and the animals are the only areas that are laid in single colors, but again the pieces are of varied sizes and laid with a minimum of special cutting.

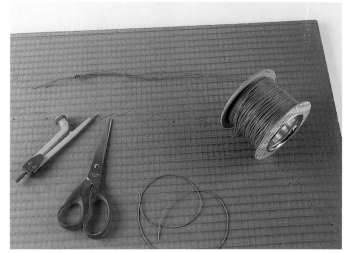

7 The lower background is laid to a slightly different pattern where the translucent pieces are offset between pairs of opaque tiles to create a different rhythm. There is also a single line of brighter color at the very top below the hills, which has great intensity because it is used in such small quantity.

8 One of the problems with fixing to tile-backer board is that it is difficult to fix hangers to the back as the material is very soft and crumbly. However, you can attach a length of fine garden wire by threading it through two pairs of holes about 2.5 cm (1 in) apart punched with a compass point. This will make two small "stitches" of wire appear on the face of the board which will spread the weight of the panel and the ends can then be wound together at the back to form a long loop to hang over a screw fixing in the wall.

9 When the tiles are all fixed to the paper and the glue is dry you are ready to fix the mosaic to the tile-backer board. First mix the grout with water into a thick paste and spread it across the back of the mosaic using your hands protected in rubber gloves, working the grout into the joints between the tiles.

10 Then sponge the back of the tiles clean with a damp tilers sponge. Make sure the sponge isn't too wet as this will wash the grout out of the joints and also make the mosaic too wet and fragile. Squeeze the sponge out and always use a clean face of the sponge for every wipe so as not to spread the grout back on to the tiles. Filling the joints with grout in this way, known as pre-grouting, stops the adhesive from coming up between the joints and also helps loosen the bond of the tiles to the paper while giving extra suction to the bond between the tiles and the adhesive.

11 Set the mosaic to one side and mix up the white cement-based adhesive to a thick paste and immediately spread onto the tile-backer board with a notched trowel to achieve an even thickness of adhesive across the surface. Make sure the wire "stitches" are covered and that the adhesive is thick enough around the vulnerable edges. Turn the pre-grouted mosaic over into the adhesive bed and press down firmly across the whole area. You can do this with your hands or using a tool such as a grouter's float or a mixing trowel, or with a flat piece of board. Keep wetting the back of the paper with a damp (but not wet) sponge until the water has penetrated and the paper turns a darker color.

12 Carefully lift an edge of the paper and, if it peels easily, continue to pull it back, parallel to the surface of the mosaic so as not to pull the tiles upwards and out of contact with the adhesive. The paper may tear into sections as you work but this is not a problem. It may be easier to take the paper off in smaller sections than in a single sheet.

13 When the paper has been removed it is important to sponge the face of the tiles clean while the grout is still wet and the excess can be lifted easily. The adhesive will also be wet so the mosaic must be treated gently. Adjustments can also be made at this stage if pieces need re-aligning slightly or recutting. When the adhesive is dry, usually in about twelve hours depending on the air temperature and humidity, the piece will need a final grout to fill in any little holes. Cover the whole area with a thick paste as before, and work it in with your fingers protected with rubber gloves. Sponge clean with a damp tiler's sponge, using a clean face for every wipe so as not to spread the grout back over the face of the tiles.

14 The final touch is to frame the panel with aluminium angle. This can be purchased at craft stores and is easily cut with a hacksaw. The corners need to be cut at a 45-degree angle, or mitered, so that they fit together neatly (because the angle is very thin the cutting does not have to be very accurate to look good on the face, and it does not matter if the corners do not fit so well on the back where they will not be seen). The angle sections can then be glued in place with a bead of silicon spread along the back face and pressed firmly onto the back of the board.

china plant pot

Mosaic does not need to be limited to flat surfaces. The curved shape of a plant pot is an ideal place for the beginner to experiment with the three-dimensional qualities of some mosaic materials. Broken china is the source of the mosaic decorating the outside of this plant pot. The design makes a feature of the molded rings found on the base of a number of similar but differently colored saucers. It is not unusual to see mosaics made from imagery painted or printed onto ceramic plates and cups, but domestic tableware has potential for a much broader range of creative uses than it is often given. The shape of objects themselves can be made to play as important a role as anything printed onto them. It can be enjoyable to experiment with effects applied to the surface of the pot or plate – embossing, sprigging, piercing or molding of the top or base of the ware, or the sculptural interest of cup handles or knobs on the lids of bowls or teapots. It is also possible to create exciting contrasts where there are no decorative motifs at all, by making a feature of the reflective or absorbent surface created by a glaze. This pot takes an aspect of ceramic tableware – the unglazed, raised, basal rim of the saucer, where the ceramic body (the color of the ceramic material itself) is revealed. The rim has been left unglazed in order to be fired easily in the kiln, but this has produced an unintentional side effect – the contrast between the color of the ceramic body and the pooling and thinning of the glaze around it, creating an inherent liveliness of color and surface. Effective design can often come from experimenting with the materials, producing ideas it would otherwise be impossible to imagine.

1 A principle that should underlie the selection of materials is an attempt to find or create similarities between them – even though at first glance they may seem thoroughly diverse. A number of different colors of saucer have been used here, but the curved rim at the base of the plates unites them all, forming a visual connection between disparate elements.

2 A flat, matte ceramic has been chosen here to act as a counterpoint to the speckly, shiny glaze with its ridged surface. Contrast is a useful tool as it emphasizes the characteristics of the material. If all the materials were shiny, a certain visual quality would be lost. To give a rhythmic continuity to the design, cut the tesserae made from the plates to a size similar to that of the ceramic. The design of the plant pot is based almost entirely around variations in the character of the line cut from the rim of the plates – variations that come from how the material has been cut and laid.

3 Earthenware pots can crack if they are left outside in freezing weather, and the same goes for earthenware plates and saucers. These saucers are made from stoneware, fired to a high temperature, making them suitable for use outside – even if the base onto which they have been stuck is more of a fragile one. The high-fired mosaic facing is not enough to ensure the pot will not crack if subjected to very low temperatures, and it should be brought inside in extreme weather conditions. Prime the terracotta pot. It is sensible to give at least two coats of primer, letting the primer dry between each application. It is advisable to mask the line at which you intend to stop the mosaic, and do not prime beyond that point, as the primer leaves a shiny surface, which is rather less attractive than the matte surface of the terracotta.

4 This design aims subliminally to echo the organic lines of branches or vegetation, so the lines created by the cut plates are laid vertically from the base of the pot. The rim of the saucer is molded in such a way that when it is used upside-down, as here, there is a cavity behind it. It is essential with any exterior mosaic, not to leave cavities, as these can easily fill with water and imperil the bonding of the mosaic. Ensure you apply a thick layer of adhesive to the back of the tile and also apply adhesive to the surface of the pot. Place the tiles firmly, pushing them down until you are certain they are well bonded. You can tell if they are by attempting to pull off a piece. The suction of the adhesive should make this very difficult to do.

5 In setting out the design, the colors of the linear tiles have been made to alternate – a gray followed by a blue. If the tiles relentlessly alternated from bottom to top, it would create rather a tedious and predictable effect. The matte tiles enhance the nature of the shiny ones and these vertical bands seem more interesting by contrasting them with some horizontal ones. The horizontal bands are laid in a contrasting color to the glazed material. As the lines spring up from the bottom, they change color as they pass through these horizontal bands. The matte ceramic tiles have been cut quite crudely in order to echo the organic fracture of the cuts in the glazed stoneware. As the pot widens towards the top, some lines are made to branch off one another, filling the space in an unpredictable way.

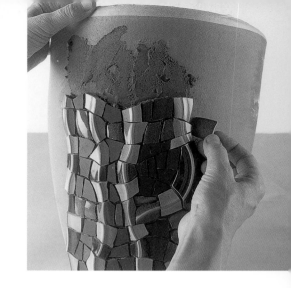

6 When the entire mosaic is complete, leave it for a day or two for the adhesive to cure to maximum strength, as the process of grouting a textured surface can be quite hard on the tiles, which need to be properly bonded before the process begins. When the mosaic surface is flat, it is quicker to use a grouting squeegee, but for a textural surface, a gloved hand is likely to be more sensitive. Rub the grout – in this case an anthracite color (match the grout color to the principal tone of the background) into the joints. With thin materials like unglazed ceramic, a superficial layer of grout is likely to penetrate to the level of the adhesive but thicker materials require a more conscious effort. Ensure this is done properly, or water may penetrate the grout, and if trapped there to freeze, may cause tiles to come off.

7 When the mosaic has been grouted, it is important to ensure the base and the rim are neatly sealed with grout. Fill the joint, carefully sponge away the excess, taking care not to remove grout from the joint itself. This final process ensures a mosaic properly protected against the elements.

tools and materials

25 cm (10 in) diameter hollow polystyrene sphere

PVA glue

Brown paper

Compass

Paintbrush

Nail

Putty Knife or small trowel

Vitreous glass tiles

Gold tiles

White cement-based adhesive

Anthracite or charcoal grout

Tiler's sponge

Garden wire

sphere

This project shows you how to create an unusual sculptural object to add color and sparkle to your garden. The sphere can be hung from the branch of a tree or laid on the ground, nestling amongst plants or at the edge of a patio amongst other objects and pots. If you made two they would look fine topping off a pair of gate posts or balustrades. It is made using the direct method and while it is a little difficult to make it does not require great skill in cutting or previous mosaic experience. The design that decorates the sphere is inspired by a mosaic in Saint Paul's chapel in Westminster Cathedral in London. The apse here is entirely covered with a starry sky executed in a beautiful mix of pale and mid-blues, combining both greenish and purplish hues together to create a very delicate and airy effect. This chapel is, itself, a reworking of the famous vault in the mausoleum of Galla Placidia in Ravenna, which features beautiful colorful stars against a deep ultramarine background. This is an interesting illustration of the influence of tradition in the art of mosaic, that does not involve exact copying but an inspired reworking of an idea to give it new life. Here the shape of the sphere makes a distant allusion to the curved surfaces of these much grander vaulted ceilings. The curved surface also means that the gold pieces are set at differing angles which allows them to catch the light and sparkle.

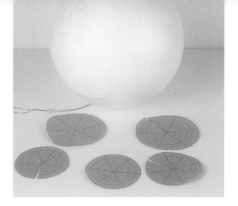

1 Glue the two halves of the sphere together using PVA glue. Use as if it were a contact adhesive by spreading a layer on each surface and allowing it to go tacky before bringing the two sides together. If you plan to hang the sphere you should insert a wire hanger with a cross piece lodged inside the sphere before assembling the two halves.

2 In order to position the stars across the surface you can cut out a series of brown paper circles of different sizes and mark them up with 5, 6 and 8 pointed stars. These can all be constructed simply with only a pencil and compass, following the rules for making pentagons, hexagons and octagons. See page 127 for further details.

3 Cutting a small segment out of each circle will help them to lie flat against the surface of the sphere. Position them on the sphere so that there is a good mix of different sizes and that they are more or less equal distances apart and draw around their perimeters with a pencil or a pen. Also mark on the circles where the points meet the edge so that you can locate the points of the stars.

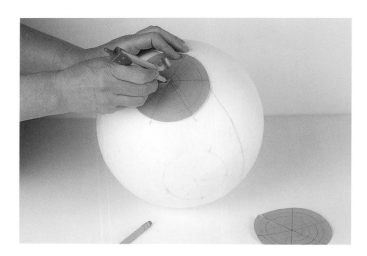

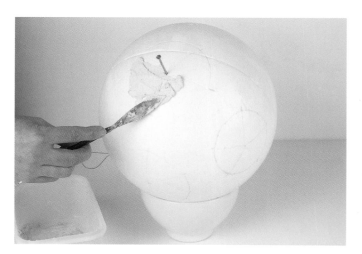

4 Mark the center of the circles, which you can do by pricking the compass point through the polystyrene. Before starting to mosaic, you will need to seal the polystyrene with a 50:50 mix of PVA and water and leave it to dry. Meanwhile you can cut some quarter tiles to make the stars with (see techniques on page 18).

5 Start by making the stars. You will need to know where the center of the star is so mark it by pushing in a small nail. Then spread adhesive over the circular area with a putty knife or small trowel, taking care not to obliterate the marks showing where the points of the stars should be. This project uses white adhesive because some of the tiles used are translucent and the white shows through and gives added sparkle.

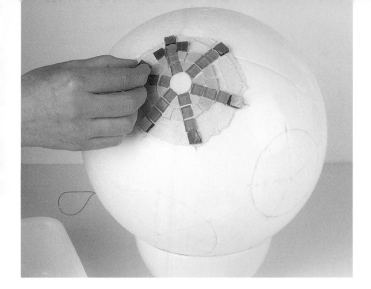 

6 Cut a circular tile for the center piece (see techniques on page 18) and remove the nail and stick the tile in place. Then lay the radiating points joining the center to the points marked around the edge. These rays do not have to be a single color but can be interrupted by gold or white dots. The idea is that each star should follow a logical pattern and all its rays should be alike and linked by concentric circles of different colors. The final circle can be of the background color so that the star's points appear to extend into the "sky" behind. All the stars use the same limited palette of white, dark green, gold, translucent green and mossy green but each star is different in the arrangement of these simple elements.

7 When all the stars are finished, fill in the background with a mix of two blues that are very close in tone but which together create an attractive flickering surface. Spread adhesive over one of the areas between the stars and lay the tiles using mostly half tiles cut at a slight angle, with a few whole tiles where possible. Follow the outlines of the circles where you can, then fill in the smaller left over areas using as large size pieces as possible so that there is an overall consistency to the sizes of the pieces throughout the background.

8 When the background is complete and the adhesive is dry you can grout the sphere. Mix the grout with water to a thick paste and apply with your hands protected in rubber gloves. Work the grout into the joints and scrape away the residue with the side of your hand. Clean the surface with a damp sponge, using a clean face of the sponge for every wipe so that you do not spread grout back over the face of the tiles.

tools and materials

30 cm (12 in) casting frame

Pair of scissors

Brown paper

Pencil

Tile nippers (side-tile biters and wheeled nippers if possible)

Washable PVA and small paintbrush

Gold and silver smalti

Vitreous glass – flat and gem

Flat-bed squeegee

2 buckets: 1 for mixing, 1 for water

Tiler's sponge

Petroleum jelly

Tissue to apply petroleum jelly

Cement colorant

Builder's sharp washed sand

Portland cement

Rubber gloves

cast fossil paver

This paver is made with vitreous glass, gold and silver and is cast into sand and cement. The slab cures gradually. The paper, onto which the mosaic tiles are stuck, is left wet for a prolonged period, causing ripples to be formed on the surface, not unlike those seen on the sand as the tide goes out. This gives a lovely naturalism to the design and ensures a slightly different result every time the piece is produced. A series of pavers can be used to make a garden path. The design is subtle and is delightful when caught by the light. The abstract, patterned elements glint, like fossils revealed in stone – an idea that works very well for a garden. Cement slurry has been used here, tinted with cement colorant.

1 Cut a piece of brown paper, matte side up, to the dimensions of the inside of the casting frame. Remove the paper from the frame.

2 Draw an oval design onto the matte (rough) side of the paper. Make a selection of colors. A number of gem tiles have been chosen, as their metallic striations pick up qualities both of the glass and the gold that accompanies them.

3 Cut the tiles into quarters and stick to the paper with washable PVA, starting from the outside of the ring. When the first, outer ring is complete, lay the inner ring of gold and silver. Each of these more precious quarter tiles has been halved. Some of the ovals alternate the blue glass on the reverse of the silver with the silver itself, some alternate the green and blue glass – the silver and gold faces shown here are the reverse of what will finally appear. The tiles in the inner third ring have also been cut into sixteenths. Complete each oval or half-oval working from the outside in. Leave to dry.

4 Use a paper towel to apply petroleum jelly as a release agent to the base and sides of the casting frame, working it well into the corners and edges. Place the paper at the base of the setting tray. Assemble the materials for casting the slab. For the slurry (which plays the same role as grout) make a mix: one part cement to one part fine, dry, sieved sand. Add cement colorant to the required tint and reserve a small portion of the dry mix as it may be needed to regrout the surface when the paver has set and the paper is removed. Add water to the remaining dry ingredients. Mix well and leave to stand for 5 minutes.

cast fossil paver

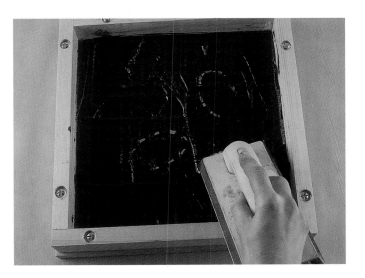

5 Apply a thin layer of cement slurry to the paper with a trowel, then remove any surplus slurry with a flat-bed squeegee, leaving as even a surface as possible.

6 While the slurry is still wet, make a mix of sand and cement: one part cement to four parts sand. Fill the setting tray with this mix and leave to cure for 48 hours. This gives the paper time to buckle and create interesting ripple forms, but the mix will still be wet enough to peel easily. Remember, before embarking on the next step, that the paver is still fragile so treat with care.

7 Unscrew the sides of the setting tray and remove. Place a board of equal size to the paver on top of it, sandwich carefully together with one hand on the top and the other on the bottom and turn over. Wet the paper with a sponge. Leave to absorb the moisture (the residue of petroleum jelly makes this process slightly trickier than usual but the glue will dissolve with persistent application of water.) Peel, clean and regrout with the reserved mixture if necessary.

tools and materials

Styrene foam block

Brown paper

Scissors

Felt tip pen

Compass

Saw

Serrated kitchen knife

Sandpaper

PVA glue

Large paintbrush

Vitreous glass tiles

Gold and silver tiles

Putty knife or small trowel

Tile nippers

Rubber gloves

Black grout

Tiler's sponge

blue cat

This three dimensional mosaic is inspired by Egyptian sculptures of the cat goddess Bast. She was a deity in Lower Egypt and was originally a lioness but after the defeat of Lower Egypt by Upper Egypt she was gradually transformed into the less ferocious domestic cat. This was not entirely a demotion as cats were highly revered in Ancient Egypt for the essential role they played in protecting the precious grain stores by controlling the potentially destructive hoards of rats and mice. They were also respected for their skill in raising their families and Bast became associated with fertility. Amulets in the form of Bast were carried both by the living and the dead, and many have been found tucked in bandages of mummified bodies. These were often made of faience, a tin-ware glaze that could be colored an intense turquoise that resembled lapis lazuli. This color is also associated with early Aztec mosaics that used the semi-precious stone itself to cover artifacts including human skulls with glittering mosaic. This sculpture is therefore influenced by the artifacts of two ancient civilizations, but at its core is a material that is a product of modern technology. This is a dense polystyrene foam that is very light, easy to cut and is stable under outdoor conditions. It is available from hardware stores and building supply stores, usually in sheet form that can be glued together to form workable blocks, and it is an excellent base for exterior mosaic sculptures. The process of covering any base with mosaic adds an extra thickness to the original form and very spindly and elongated shapes are hard to achieve neatly. Even in this project the process has transformed the elegant polystyrene sculpture of an Egyptian deity into a more homely and domestic blue cat.

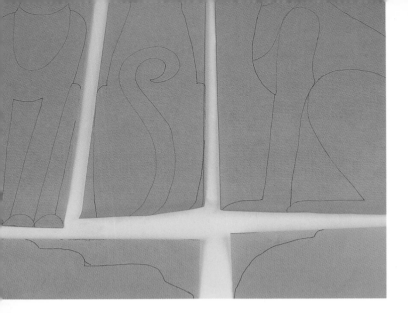

1 Cut out rectangles of brown paper the same size as all the sides of your block of polystyrene. Draw on the shape of the cat from the appropriate viewpoint, i.e. front view, side view, back view. You can enlarge and trace these from the templates on page 127.

2 Cut around the outline of the shapes with scissors.

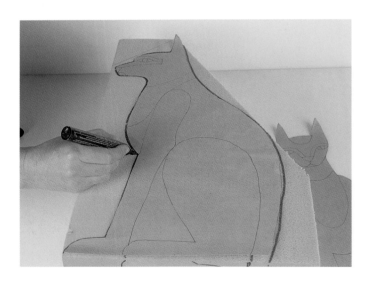

3 Place the paper shapes on the polystyrene block and draw around the outline with a felt tip pen.

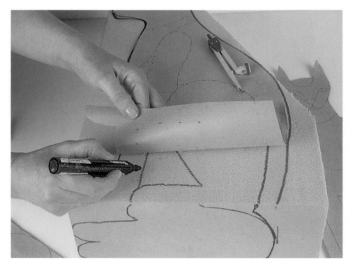

4 To mark the inner lines make pin pricks through the paper along the line with about 2.5 cm (1 in) spaces between pricks using the point of a compass. Lift the paper and draw a line in felt tip pen joining up the holes.

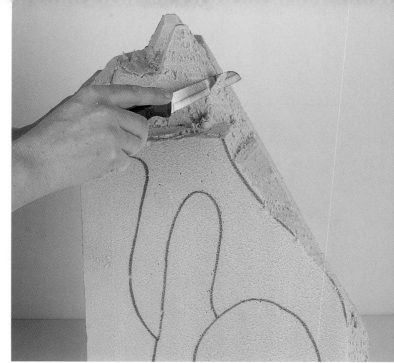

5 Start to carve away at the block. To begin with you can remove large pieces of foam with a saw, using the drawings on the side as guide for which parts need to be removed.

6 More detailed cutting will have to be done with a smaller tool, such as a serrated kitchen knife. To achieve the three dimensional form you will quite quickly cut away the original lines on the outside face of the block but you can always draw on new lines as you work. Try to carve out an approximate block-like shape to start with before trying to achieve any fine detail, but do not worry if you accidentally cut away too much as the foam sticks back together very well with PVA glue. The most difficult areas are where the foam is cut away to form a recess, for instance on the side between the back and front leg. It is difficult to maneuver the blade into any position that will allow a clean cut, but the foam is so soft it can be hacked away in lumps with the point of the knife.

7 Rough areas can be rubbed down with coarse sandpaper, but again some of the recesses will be difficult to reach. However, it will be possible to even out these surfaces with the adhesive layer, so long as the overall surface is lower than the finished surface needs to be.

8 Prime the surface of the polystyrene with a 20:80 solution of PVA to water. As well as reducing the absorbency of the surface this will help to fix down any loose fragments of foam.

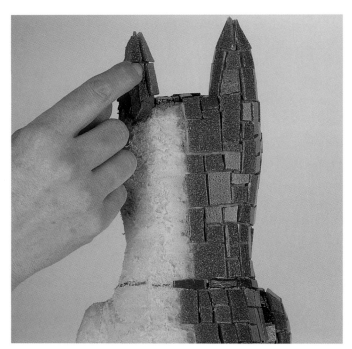

9 When the foam form is finished you can draw on details such as the eyes, the tail and the position of the necklace. You can then start sticking by applying a small area of adhesive in a thin layer to the foam base with a putty knife or small trowel and applying the mosaic pieces. The general rule is to avoid very small pieces as they have less chance of sticking, and you will also find that where the form curves you will have to lay the tiles so that the joints follow the line of the curve rather than trying to span across it.

10 The most difficult areas of laying are the ears where there is no alternative but to use a series of small tapering triangles clustering up to the point. It is easier to start at the top of the ears with long triangles bedded in plenty of adhesive, and then work downwards to the base, trying not to knock off the top pieces as you go.

11 The tail can be made up of angled halves to form a curve and some lines picked out in quarters. The main areas are laid in a mixture of halves, wholes, quarters and rectangles of different shapes and sizes. This approach does not emphasise any one direction over another and makes it easy to cover irregular shapes without creating awkward junctions. The recessed areas between the legs are laid in the same way but in a darker color. Keep repositioning the piece so that it is at a comfortable level to reach without disturbing areas you have already fixed.

12 When all the tiles are stuck down and the adhesive is completely dry the piece can be grouted. This is best done by applying the grout with your hands protected in rubber gloves. Work the grout into the joints and scrape off as much excess as you can with the side of your hand.

13 Clean off the grout immediately with a damp sponge using a clean face for every wipe so as not to spread the grout back over the face of the tiles. Where the grout collects in some of the recesses and around the eyes it can be scraped away with a small tool. As the piece dries, and preferably before it is completely dry, any residue of grout on the surface can be rubbed down with a dry rag.

30 cm (12 in) casting frame

2 buckets: 1 for mixing, 1 for water

Screwdriver

Trowel for mixing

Flat-bed squeegee

Petroleum jelly

Silver sand

Builder's sharp washed sand

Cement

Slate – 1 bag pink, 1 bag green

Black marble pebbles

Piece of hardboard or similar

slate paver

This paver uses slate in a decorative way, on edge, so the depth of the slate is gripped by the sand and cement. The design is laid at the bottom of the frame, pressed into a wet silver sand. Once complete, wet sand and cement is laid over it until it is dry when the slab is turned and the completed design is revealed. The silver sand is a working bed, holding the pieces as the paver is laid – material that is too thin will not be held properly and may fall out. Every piece needs to be pushed through until it touches the base of the casting frame, but nothing should be submerged or there will be nothing to hold it in place as the paver is turned. This design has an almost floral quality. The large pieces are hard to cut – designs are most successful it they go where the material leads, but as the pieces of slate are generally long and narrow, there is an immense range of creative possibilities.

1 Assemble the casting frame, making sure all sides are securely screwed into place. Apply petroleum jelly as a release agent. Take care to work it well into the corners and edges. Mix silver sand with enough water to ensure it is damp enough to hold stones placed into it firmly in position. Place a layer of about 1 cm (⅜ in) depth evenly across the base.

2 Select the material, and wash thoroughly in a bucket to remove all traces of dust. Reserve the bucket of water in which the stones were washed and let it stand for 24 hours before pouring the clear liquid down the drain and placing the stone-dusty sludge in a bag for disposal. Place the two colors of slate and the marble pebbles in boxes ready to place into the frame. Start by laying the black marble centers of the flower-like structures and lay the flower-like shapes around them. Remember the side that will finally be exposed is the side you press into the sandy mixture. Continue laying the stones until the frame is full.

3 Pour a slurry of cement over the slate, to act as a grout (two parts cement to one part fine sieved sand). Allow it to flow into the interstices between the stones. It is prevented from flowing to the bottom and marring the face of the stone by the bed of silver sand into which everything has been laid.

slate paver

4 Make a mix of sand and cement (one part cement to four parts sand). Mix the dry components in a bucket, make a well in the center, then add enough water to achieve a butter icing-like consistency. Mix well, and fill the casting frame to the top. Take a flat-bed squeegee and tap the surface flat. Leave to dry for about a week.

5 Unscrew the edges from the casting frame. Take a piece of hardboard and place on top of the cast slab. Grip the base and the hardboard on top of the frame firmly between your hands, and turn over the slab. If you do not sandwich the board firmly enough, the slab may fall out. Carefully remove the large base of the casting frame. The layer of silver sand makes this an easy task to do.

6 Brush away the sand and the design is revealed and ready to bed into position outside. Although the slate may look vulnerable, it will be perfectly sound, unless the bed of sand was was too thick.

templates

Enlarge or reduce on the photocopier as required.

House number (pages 28–31)

Bird bath (pages 48–53)

Flying jay wall plaque (pages 76–79)

Enlarge to 30 x 30 cm (12 x 12 in)

Night and day roundel (pages 64–69)
Enlarge so diameter is 52 cm (20 in)

Runner bean (pages 84–89)
Enlarge so diameter is 39 cm (15 in)

Two beasts under a tree (pages 94–99)
Enlarge to 48 x 48 cm (19 x 19 in)

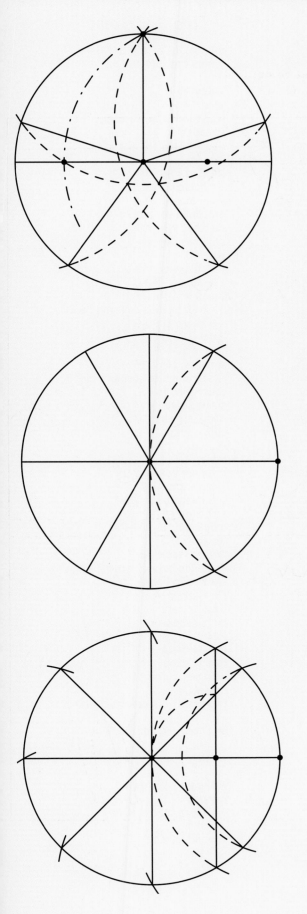

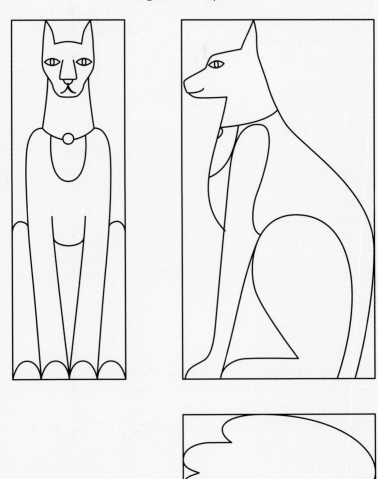

Blue cat (pages 112–117)
Enlarge to the required size

Sphere (pages 104–107)
Enlarge so diameter is 25 cm (10 in)

BAREFOOT

Escape on the Underground Railroad

by Pamela Duncan Edwards

illustrated by Henry Cole

 HarperCollins*Publishers*

For Alistair with thanks for the invaluable critiquing
of my stories. With love and pride
—P. D. E.

For Charlotte
—H. C.

The illustrations in this book were painted with acrylic paints and
colored pencils on Arches Hot Press watercolor paper.

Library of Congress Cataloging-in-Publication Data
Edwards, Pamela Duncan.
  Barefoot / by Pamela Duncan Edwards ; illustrated by Henry Cole.
    p.   cm.
  Summary: A group of animals help a runaway slave escape his pursuers.
  ISBN 0-06-027137-X. — ISBN 0-06-027138-8 (lib. bdg.)
  ISBN 0-06-443519-9 (pbk.)
  [1. Fugitive slaves—Fiction.   2. Afro-Americans—Fiction.   3. Animals—Fiction.]
1. Cole, Henry, ill. II. Title.
PZ7.E26365Bar 1997   95-44863
[E]—dc20   CIP
                                                  AC

Typography by David Neuhaus and Elynn Cohen
13 SCP 20 19 18 17 16
❖
Visit us on the World Wide Web!
http://www.harperchildrens.com